Simple Autism Strategies
for Home and School

Simple Autism Strategies for Home and School

Practical Tips, Resources and Poetry

Sarah Cobbe

Foreword by Glenys Jones

Jessica Kingsley *Publishers*
London and Philadelphia

First published in 2019
by Jessica Kingsley Publishers
73 Collier Street
London N1 9BE, UK
and
400 Market Street, Suite 400
Philadelphia, PA 19106, USA

www.jkp.com

Copyright © Sarah Cobbe 2019
Foreword copyright © Glenys Jones 2019

Front cover illustration by Michelle Rebello-Tindall

Library of Congress Cataloging in Publication Data
A CIP catalog record for this book is available from the Library of Congress

British Library Cataloguing in Publication Data
A CIP catalogue record for this book is available from the British Library

ISBN 978 1 78592 444 6
eISBN 978 1 78450 817 3
Printed and bound by CPI Group (UK) Ltd, Croydon, CR0 4YY

To my parents, Gerry and Sian.

CONTENTS

FOREWORD

Over the 70 years since autism was first mentioned in the literature, views on how it is understood have developed and changed in the light of research and discussion. Many interventions have been developed to address specific areas such as communication and social understanding or to develop understanding and skills more broadly. Research on what makes a difference to autistic children and adults and their families is difficult, not least because the autistic population is diverse and so what might help one child may not be suitable or appropriate for another. Sample sizes are often small and the research design, methods and outcomes measured often mean that results are inconclusive or not very helpful for a parent or teacher living with or working with a specific child (see the National Institute for Health and Care Excellence Guidance, Clinical Guidance 170).

So, currently, parents and teaching staff rely mostly on their own judgement as to what is likely to help. This is based on their knowledge of the individual child concerned and their past experience, and expertise gained from their own reading or training. However, as parents and teaching staff have access to many different sources of information either from their own research online or from the literature and from the people involved with the child, what they receive in terms of knowledge and understanding is very varied. Some information may be useful but other ideas may be misleading or inaccurate, or not relevant to their child. So, this book is an excellent resource as the ideas within it have been developed over several years by the author in her work with autistic children and their families. Strategies which she has found effective at school and at home are described and further references given to related resources devised by others.

What is true is that the people who live and work with an autistic child or adult are the most important resource. How they understand and relate to the individual is key. What parents and teaching staff do in practice will be linked to how they view autism generally and what their main objectives are. Increasingly, parents and teaching staff are being urged to ask the autistic child or adult for their perspective on what might be helpful. This book fits well with this position. It sets out everyday dilemmas for parents and teaching staff at home and school and aims to illustrate the likely perspective of the autistic child. Suggestions are made as to why an autistic child might act differently from other children, using current understandings of autism with reference to the most recent diagnostic criteria in the *Diagnostic and Statistical Manual of Mental Disorders, version 5*, or *DSM-5* (American Psychiatric Association 2013) (*What we can learn*). A range of ideas is given on what might be helpful if the child's actions are deemed to be a barrier to further learning or when they affect other people adversely (*How we can help*).

This book will be equally useful for parents and teaching staff alike as it has distinct and customised sections for both groups. That said, both groups would benefit from reading the whole book to consider the issues that might occur at home and at school and the strategies that might be helpful that can be used across both settings.

Sarah has worked as a teacher within special schools and as part of an autism advisory team, and was diagnosed herself, in adulthood, as being on the autism spectrum. In her youth, she also worked with autistic adults. In constructing and writing this book, she is therefore able to draw on her personal experience of being autistic and on her discussions with parents and staff, her own training, and her classroom practice. She has found poetry a useful way of capturing the perspective and dilemmas experienced by autistic children and adults and uses her own poems very effectively to introduce some of the key topics. A key strength of the book is the wealth of references that Sarah has included, directing the reader to specific chapters or sections related to the topic (*Where we can go next*). Through these and the ideas suggested in this book, readers are likely to add to and modify their understanding of autism and the strategies they adopt, leading to more effective practice and better outcomes for all concerned.

Dr Glenys Jones, Autism Centre for Education
and Research, University of Birmingham

ACKNOWLEDGEMENTS

This book has been more than a year in the making and my thanks go to:

* Jessica Kingsley Publishers for helping me fulfil a career-long aspiration

* The editors Simeon Hance and James Cherry for developing the structure and content of the manuscript

* Dr Glenys Jones for writing the foreword and reviewing the manuscript

* Amy Challenor for some useful tips in the area of speech and language therapy

* All of the parents, professionals and children I have worked with during my career. You have inspired some of the themes and ideas in this book and continue to teach me a great deal.

DISCLAIMER

The strategies and resources described in the book are drawn from my own research and experiences in the field of autism, and from discussions I have had with parents and fellow professionals. The advice provided in each section is written to the best of my knowledge, and assumes that any person acting on it will make the necessary preparations to ensure that the chosen strategies and resources are relevant and appropriate, and used safely with all children. The author is not responsible for any damages, losses or subsequent health concerns. This book is not intended to be used as a diagnostic tool nor for medical advice and the reader is advised to seek support from the relevant services and professionals if such information is required. As far as I am aware, statements and quotes within the text have been recorded and referenced accurately and any errors will be corrected in future reprints. Please note that the citation of websites, products, books, journals and media clips is for informational rather than promotional purposes – provided only with the intention of signposting interested readers. Please also note that the availability and details of the sources may be subject to change or have changed since the book went to press.

INTRODUCTION

In the midst of a perennial search for *another* important and misplaced piece of paper, my family recently discovered a booklet of poems that I wrote when I was 12 years old. While the poems were a poignant reminder of how I viewed friends and family as a young girl, they were also proof of a long-standing interest in writing about other people. Indeed, several decades have passed and I'm still writing poems about people, but now most notably about people on the autism spectrum. Autism is a fascinating condition and has an undeniable draw. Once you experience autism – whether that's personally or from a distance – you can't let it go. There is just *something* about a child with autism that catches you unawares, that impels you to watch and wonder what she or he is thinking in that instant; it's a fascination as powerful to me today as it was during my early experiences of autism.

My introduction to autism followed my university graduation in the late 1990s, starting with a job in the south of England supporting adults with autism in a residential home. It was a premier insight into some of the challenges and highlights of life on the autism spectrum – and it left me with indelibly fond memories. The adults I worked with were remarkable people and will forever form the roots of my lifelong passion for improvement. For as much as I'd like to think I have helped the hundreds of children, parents and professionals in the jobs that have followed, I know that they have helped me more. I can honestly say that my work has taught me more about human nature and my own capabilities than anything else to date. Certainly, my idea of what should be considered 'normal' has changed over the years, in both academic and everyday contexts.

Children on the autism spectrum have a great deal to teach us and should never be underestimated. I believe the more we stop, look and listen to them, the more we appreciate the value of our own communications, relationships and aspirations. Unfortunately, those of you who already have links with autism will know that not everyone understands or appreciates this – despite the growing awareness of its presence among us all. A recent survey by The National Autistic Society, for instance, reported that while 99.5 per cent of people in the UK had heard of autism, only 16 per cent of autistic people and their families felt that the general public understood its impact on behaviour (The National Autistic Society 2016). This goes some way to explaining the motivation for my book.

It is my intention to spread a little of my knowledge and experiences of life on the autism spectrum – through poetry – to give the reader a flavour of what this can be like and how to help. Poetry, I'll admit, may not seem like an obvious or practical place for us to start. Indeed, if your instinctive response to poetry stems from memories of indecipherable lessons at school, you might be thinking that it is too niche, abstract and intangible to address a condition as kaleidoscopic, real and tangible as autism – that poetry couldn't *possibly* have scope to unpick the challenges currently playing out in your classroom or household. Bear with me. I think poetry does have relevance and I will try to explain why.

WHAT POETRY CAN OFFER

In recent years, I have discovered that the act of writing poetry is personally therapeutic and sometimes cathartic. On the days when the world and its demands are high and resilience is low, poems act like a counterweight to overloading. If I'm concentrating on the rules defining a particular type of poem, then I'm only thinking about this and have an outlet for articulating something on my mind. Sometimes a poem – like a haiku[1] – is the simplest way to say or explain a difficult thing, or, as John Paul Lederach eloquently puts it, a means of 'trying to capture the full complexity of human experience in the fewest words possible'.[2] As a prime example, in the hours it took me to write the final paragraphs of this introduction, I can summarise that process in a poem that consumed barely a few minutes:

> *whenever I write*
> *a haiku, scrambled thoughts find*
> *release in penned words*

Poetry, then, can turn intricate thoughts or ideas into words and express them in a succinct way, making it easier for the 'speaker' to engage with a reader. Krista Tippett[3] talks about poetry as a forum for conversation and considered as such, makes poetry an interesting metaphor for communicating with someone who has autism – someone who struggles with their ability to process information, make themselves understood and to understand

---

1   A haiku consists of three lines and seventeen syllables in a pattern of five, seven and five

2   Taken from an interview transcript involving Krista Tippett and John Paul Lederach, which was recorded on 8 July 2010. Accessed on 23/03/18 at https://onbeing.org/programs/john-paul-lederach-art-peace

3   Taken from an interview transcript involving Krista Tippett and Naomi Shihab Nye, which was recorded as a podcast on 28 July 2016. Accessed on 23/03/18 at https://onbeing.org/programs/naomi-shihab-nye-your-life-is-a-poem

other people. It helps me envisage each poem as a metaphorical conversation starter, where the child with autism communicates through the written word and the listener responds (i.e., by reading). The poem articulates what the child finds difficult to say and ensures that their voice is heard without interruption; a listener can interrupt words in speech but a reader can't interrupt words in a poem.

I believe, therefore, that the poetry in my book has relevance in two ways: as an art that we can use to communicate and interpret the thoughts and experiences of children with autism, and as a concept with analogous features. The poems I have written, for example, have a natural rhythm and repetition to them; many children with autism welcome rhythm and repetition. The poems have been written in a range of styles[4] and these are congruent with the range of profiles within the spectrum. Plus, I have already alluded to the fact that poetry exists in different forms bound by different rules and conventions – essentially describing aspects of daily life – so it does not take a great leap in thought to relate this to life within or outside the spectrum today. We *all* experience life as a collection of events and experiences, and are all programmed to interpret and respond to these in our own way. Indeed, the poet Naomi Shihab Nye[5] suggests that life itself is a poem because the word poem could describe any moment where we find ourselves thinking and reflecting on something we can see, or have seen and done. So, next time you find yourself lost for words over a beautiful vista or a difficult problem, try considering the virtues of poetry. The very idea might amuse or even inspire you – after

---

4   Styles include my interpretation of those known as concrete, haiku, rhyme royal, sonnet, tetractys, double tetractys, pantoum, tanka, epigram, clerihew, ghazal and cinquain

5   Taken from an interview transcript involving Krista Tippett and Naomi Shihab Nye, which was recorded as a podcast on 28 July 2016. Accessed on 23/03/18 at https://onbeing.org/programs/naomi-shihab-nye-your-life-is-a-poem

all, Stephen Fry (2005) suggests that poetry resides in everyone. Perhaps it just reverberates deeper in some of us than others. Just like autism.

WHO THIS BOOK IS FOR

This book should appeal to anyone who has a personal connection with autism, and particularly someone whose primary role is as a parent, carer or relative, or as a teacher, support assistant or professional. These audiences were very much in mind as I wrote the book, thinking about the people I have encountered in my work and the children I have seen in schools. One of my main goals was to produce something that was accessible and engaging, something that would strike a chord with readers and potentially remind them of something they have seen, heard or experienced. It was also my intention to write the poems in the first person so we could consider some of the possible motivations for the various and visible manifestations of autism, hypothetically, through the child's eyes. Autism, as we shall see, is sometimes referred to as an invisible disability but the associated behaviours are not. Often, our first impression of autism is based on what we see rather than what the individual is communicating – something that might resonate with the author and parent Henry Normal (Normal and Pell 2018, p.50), who cites Alain de Botton when remarking on the fact that 'we view ourselves from the inside but others from the outside'. If you want to help someone, then it helps to think about the 'why' not just the 'what'. I hope that this is what you will gain from your reading, that by the time you have finished the book you will have a greater insight into the strengths, needs and interests of children on the autism spectrum and – as shown by your subsequent actions – a greater influence on those you support, teach or parent.

HOW TO USE THIS BOOK

How you use the book will obviously depend on your circumstances and motivations, which are likely to be as diverse and variable as the spectrum itself. I am aware that some issues will be more relevant to one reader than to another but this potentially widens the draw of the book, since it contains information on a reasonably broad range of topics and the topics are easily located. Of further note is the flexibility afforded by the book's construction, because you can choose to read some, most or all of the material at any point and it won't matter if parts or chapters are read out of order. What should matter, however, is your starting point in any of the topics. This should always be the poem.

The book contains 93 poems, which are grouped into three parts and 36 short chapters. Every part begins with an introduction defining its subject area and this provides a context for the chapters that follow. Part 1 focuses on the profiles and characteristics associated with the autism spectrum, Part 2 studies aspects of time in school, while Part 3 explores aspects of life at home. Every chapter has a name identifying its theme and consists of one or more poems, which represent a particular topic. You could think of the chapter as the heading and any poem as a sub-heading. If you were interested in the way that children on the spectrum communicate, for instance, you could look in Part 1 at Chapter 9: Conversation Skills and find three poems representing reciprocity, talking in groups and blunt speech. I should point out, however, that many – but not all – of the poems have a title as well as a sub-heading but that their titles are listed in the text rather than in the contents pages (to make referencing simpler). The poem concerning talking in groups, for example, is actually called 'Heated Conversations'.

Information supporting the poems is divided into three sections: 'What we can learn', 'How we can help' and 'Where we can go next' – collectively providing the reader with an interpretation of the poem, three possible strategies, and two sources for further reading or application. The information is not exhaustive by any means but should be a useful starting point. While it may strike the more experienced readers that some of the more obvious ideas have been overlooked in places, I wish to point out that this has been deliberate to avoid undue repetition in the writing.

To get the most out of the poems, I invite you to read them out loud – a practice that I know Stephen Fry is particularly keen on – and to read them twice (before the interpretation and after it)! Not only will this make the poems more memorable, but it should also deepen your appreciation for the messages they convey from a first-person perspective. Some readers might think I have been presumptuous in assuming the thoughts and feelings of people with a diagnosis, but I'd like to think that my observations are a reasonable interpretation of behaviours I have encountered in my work. In most cases, the poems are based on imaginary children but this does not diminish their worth as they are still reminiscent of things I have personally experienced – or are a whisper of stories that professionals and parents have shared with me along the way. The exceptions are only in those that relate to me and my own diagnosis of autism.

However you read the book and however you use it though, my ultimate wish is for it to enhance your own experiences and views of life for children with autism – children who face challenges big and small every day, but who don't necessarily experience or manage them in 'expected' ways. Whether you are a parent, a professional or a relative, and whether you have a diagnosis or not, there is perhaps something here for us all to learn. I've enjoyed writing this book and hope you enjoy reading it.

SOME TERMINOLOGY

Before we begin, I feel the need to explain a little vocabulary. Most of you will have already realised that the terminology surrounding autism can be just as complex or puzzling as the actual profile of behaviours. As soon as you begin researching or reading, you soon encounter a confusing mix of labels: Asperger syndrome, atypical autism, autism spectrum condition/s (ASC), autism spectrum disorder/s (ASD), childhood autism, high functioning autism, pathological demand avoidance (PDA), pervasive developmental disorder, or the autism/autistic spectrum. Broadly speaking, each term is equivalent to another or a subtle variation of it. I like to think of them as a family of words comprising siblings, twins and relatives. Deciding who or what you talk about is essentially a matter of context, timing, preference or clinical persuasion. If I were to be precise, however, I would need to tell you that the clinical diagnosis individuals now receive is most likely to be autism spectrum disorder (ASD),[6] not autism.

A diagnosis of ASD arises from the recognition of certain categories of traits, which vary widely from one person to the next – explaining why we use the word 'spectrum' or the description 'on the autism spectrum'. Talk of ASD can prompt confusion not least because various professionals – including me – prefer the abbreviation ASC (referring to a condition rather than a disorder) but continue to use the word autism overall.

---

6   The American Psychiatric Association produces a diagnostic manual that covers a wide range of conditions. The current edition is called the *Diagnostic and Statistical Manual of Mental Disorders, version 5 (DSM-5)* and was published in 2013. *DSM-5* redefined the diagnoses of conditions relating to autism and pulled these together under the new heading of autism spectrum disorder (see The National Autistic Society 2016). This convention is similarly described in the manual produced by the World Health Organisation, the *International Classification of Diseases (ICD-11)* (see Autism-Europe 2018).

Added to this confusion is the fact that autism often has a dual meaning in modern times: it can be discussed as one of three distinctive profiles *and* mean the autism spectrum.[7] This is confusing maybe, but not that surprising given the vagaries of the English language and its bountiful homonyms (those words with the same spelling and pronunciation, but different meanings). In this vein, a person can show the traits identified with autism, Asperger syndrome or PDA and simultaneously be regarded as a person with ASC, and on the autism spectrum. Each profile will share similar traits but appear different. These traits were once regarded as a Triad of Impairments.[8]

Text phrases

For the sake of simplicity, I will use the word autism as a generic term encompassing all that is described within the spectrum, but sometimes refer to autism as one of the profiles, along with PDA and Asperger syndrome. These distinctions, however, should be comprehensible where they occur. When I talk about children in the poems, I may alternate between the following terms: she, he, they, an autist, a child/children with autism, an autistic child/children, a child/children on the spectrum, or simply, the autism spectrum. I have no desire to reject political correctness – you may or may not like these terms – but will excuse myself by noting that my efforts are well intentioned and designed for reading variety. It would feel somewhat cumbersome to only

---

7   The National Autistic Society, for instance, talks about autism, pathological demand avoidance and Asperger syndrome (see The National Autistic Society (2016) *What is Autism?* www.autism.org.uk/about/what-is.aspx)

8   Lorna Wing provided the idea of an autism spectrum and formulated The Triad of Impairments with Judith Gould in the late 1970s. This refers to social impairments in the areas of interaction, communication and imagination (Donvan and Zucker 2016)

ever refer to the individual as a 'child with autism'. My preference will also be for the pronoun 'she' but this should not be mistaken as a fact that the poem or situation is only relevant to girls. In some cases, this will be true, but in most it won't – we know that autism affects both males and females.

PART 1

THE AUTISM SPECTRUM

The autism spectrum has a longer history than you might realise. We can easily refer back to the 1940s to read about the set of behaviours that the clinicians Leo Kanner and Hans Asperger described but it would be naive to think that the behaviours themselves first appeared at this time. What we now classify as autistic behaviours, for example, have long been proffered as explanations for the achievements of individuals such as Isaac Newton, Thomas Jefferson and Albert Einstein (James 2016), or at least been recognised in descriptions of people in the past, including Victor, The Wild Boy of Aveyron.[1] Even the nature of 'autistic thinking' was noted by the Swiss psychiatrist Eugen Bleuler more than a century ago (Donvan and Zucker 2016, p.40). And doubtless, there are many among you who can think back to secondary school and wonder – knowing what you know now – if autism would have been a good fit for the classmate you recall as quirky or aloof.

So autism in form, if not name, has been around for a long time. To my mind, the behaviours diagnosed by contemporary

---

1   Victor of Aveyron (c.1788–1828) was a young French boy who was found at the age of around 12. His developmental delay and apparent difficulties with education and language have subsequently led to speculation that he was autistic

professionals are not vastly different to those described by Kanner and Asperger; the evolutions are more apparent in the terminology and public conceptions. In the 1890s, for instance, children could be defined as feeble minded or as imbeciles and even, in the 1940s, considered handicapped within the boundaries of delicate, educationally sub-normal and maladjusted (Hodkinson 2016) – terms that seem clinical, unethical and shocking with the wisdom of hindsight. But perhaps we should not be too complacent; they were, after all, accepted in their time. Will the many terms we have at our disposal remain politically correct in the decades to come? Even now, the words 'normal' and 'typical' can be inflammatory, and advocates in various quarters already discuss the spectrum as a concept embedded in neurodiversity rather than a pigeonhole in society.

> With all that we have begun to learn in recent decades about the intricacy and idiosyncrasy of 'normal' brains and minds...I hope...society will find ways to make best use of the talents and energies of differently able minds... (Tammet 2009, p.362)

It's ironic that a condition comprising the need for sameness and inflexible thinking is in itself continuously subject to change and open to interpretation. Will there come a point thus when the diagnosis collapses under its own weight of restrictiveness or breadth? And is this the most important argument? Perhaps the 'correctness' of diagnosis should focus on the *person*, not the terms – ultimately the means of respecting, understanding and addressing an individual's needs and strengths. Steve Silberman's (2015) book *NeuroTribes*, for instance, has a strapline urging readers to 'think smarter about people who think differently'. With luck, I have illustrated a little of this in my poetry.

Chapter 1

DIAGNOSIS

1. Diagnosing Doubts
(A poem about sharing the diagnosis)

How do I cope with these worries and fears?
These thoughts that temper my teenage years.

What if I am? What if I'm not?
How will professionals explain the issues I've got?
Why is the normal box papered with doubt?
What if it's opened and the spectrum falls out?

What we can learn

Pause for a moment to consider what the diagnosis of autism means to you. Imagine seeing it writ large on a road sign. Metaphorically, are you at a crossroad or a blind corner? Inching down a country lane or speeding on a motorway? Have you arrived at the scene of a crash or reached the airport with a new destination in sight? Autism means different things to different families, but in most cases will be considered a life-changing event. It's one thing to believe you or your child has a diagnosis but something else to know it – for some families it can be felt first as a bereavement, a disappointment or a failure. These feelings and others are captured in an article written by Emily Perl Kingsley called 'Welcome to Holland'.[1] The article uses the act of going on holiday as a metaphor for parents coming to terms with their child's disability: travelling to Italy and then discovering that the plane has been re-routed to Holland. Emily proposes that the ensuing confusion, frustration, loss and disappointment will be replaced by calm, acceptance and enjoyment. Whatever we think about autism – seeking, doubting, accepting or avoiding the diagnosis – it is here to stay. The word and its derivatives have been around for a long time and its behaviours longer still. Our poem presents us with a child in her teenage years, not yet diagnosed and agonising over its uncertainty. In the event that she is diagnosed, we can only imagine how *she* will come to terms with it, let alone her family. I think it is important that children who have the capacity to understand their diagnosis *know* about their diagnosis. Not everyone will agree with me. I would, however, encourage people to think not only about the disadvantages of sharing the diagnosis but the very real advantages too.

How we can help

1. When it comes to sharing the diagnosis with your child, don't underestimate the importance of timing. It's not just about when you and your child are relaxed or how long you think the conversation will last. The 'right' time should initially involve consideration of her age and level of understanding as well as consideration of how prepared and ready you are to deal with her responses.

---

1   Emily has a son with Down syndrome and writes for the programme *Sesame Street*. Her article can be accessed via this link: https://en.m.wikipedia.org/wiki/Emily_Kingsley. The *Sesame Street* programme now features a character with autism called Julia, who joined the show in 2017, and the website contains a range of autism resources for parents: http://autism.sesamestreet.org

2. There are plenty of resources and strategies available for explaining diagnosis. What works for one person will vary for another, but in most cases will include some sort of visual resource – something that children can see. Remember that an autism diagnosis includes difficulty listening to, processing and responding to *spoken* information. I tend to use stories with young children and mainly drawing and guided worksheets with older children. When it comes to teenagers, I usually recommend books and websites for their parents to share with them before they meet me, and then use this as a way of opening our conversation.

3. Some parents may feel daunted by the prospect of explaining the diagnosis to their child and worry about getting it wrong. Try to treat it as you would any important or sensitive conversation with your child and think about what you are going to say in advance. It may sound a little odd to use an analogy when we know that children can take things literally (we should still be mindful of that), but I often find that making a connection between the person's diagnosis and some aspect of their character or anxieties makes the content more tangible. It's quite common, for example, to use a computer analogy to talk about the brain's wiring, or traffic jams to talk about sensory overload.

Where we can go next

* Elder, J. (2006) *Different Like Me. My Book of Autism Heroes.* London and Philadelphia, PA: Jessica Kingsley Publishers
  A book showcasing people past and present who have made significant contributions to society in areas such as maths, science and art – people who have made a difference by being different and quite possibly autistic.

✳ Miller, A. (2018) *All About Me. A Step-by-Step Guide to Telling Children and Young People on the Autism Spectrum about Their Diagnosis*. London and Philadelphia, PA: Jessica Kingsley Publishers

This book is divided into two parts that essentially focus on the preparatory steps for sharing the diagnosis and the ways of teaching the person about their condition. The first part includes a helpful section describing arguments for and against sharing the diagnosis with children, while the second part includes a section demonstrating how people can make explanations of autism accessible to different individuals.

Chapter 2

AUTISM PROFILES

2. All About Me
(A poem about the characteristics of autism)

I like my own space and don't like to mix
People make problems I don't want to fix.
Their eyes and their mouths don't make any sense
Being social with others is extremely intense.

I like to make sounds and my words can be few
It's not always so easy to make small talk with you.
I need objects and photos, symbols or signs
And one on one sessions with processing time.

I like days with order, full of routines
So I know what I'm doing and what everything means.
Warn me of changes and I'll manage alright
Spring things upon me and I'll show you my fright.

I line up my books and all of my bears
Always in rows and never in pairs.
Don't touch them or change them or spoil the neat line
Things kept in their place means everything's fine.

I have really strong senses – they're like super powers

But they can overwhelm – like cars at rush hour.
So stims give me focus and help me feel calm
And shut out the panic, the fear and alarm.

They tell me I'm different, that I've got A-S-C but
What does that mean? I'm just being me.
Not one in a hundred. That mustn't be true
Cos I'm one in a million for all that I do.

What we can learn

You could say this is a poem of autism averages – neatly boxing a spectrum's worth of traits and behaviours into six verses. Except it isn't and it doesn't. I've used sections of this poem in a number of my training sessions but only to demonstrate the sheer breadth of the spectrum. It means different things to different people, whether you are looking inwards to your own version of autism or looking outwards at someone diagnosed with it. I always make the point that what I am presenting in my training can never be fully comprehensive. How a communication difficulty is manifest in one person will contrast with its presentation in another; similarly for sensory processing difficulties, interaction skills and patterns of restricted behaviour. Little wonder it can be confusing for people new to autism, trying to make sense of the diagnosis or diagnostic criteria, relating this to the child in their care and then trying to work out which strategy is needed at any point. I like this poem because it *suggests* what autism may be like and compels us to find out more. It also suggests that autism encompasses a wide range of behaviours, which can be triggered or harnessed depending on their management and whether people understand and respect what these mean. In this vein, the poem also demonstrates that autism is only as 'limiting' as the environment and our resources, or our capacity and our perspective.

How we can help

1. In my mind, it is vital that anyone supporting a child on the spectrum has at least a basic understanding of how autism may present *before* putting strategies into place. That way you are more prepared to understand the issue or concern and can be more effective in your support. It's like doing the edges of the jigsaw before trying to tackle the middle – the first steps give the picture structure.

2. Very often it seems that children's behaviour improves as their communication skills develop – so teaching and supporting communication is essential. Communication should be an interactive process, so ensure that you give children the means, opportunities and reasons to communicate with you; don't only consider how *you* are going to communicate with them.

3. I regularly meet people who are completely new to autism and worry that their inexperience will make a given situation or issue worse – as if there is only one way to manage with a behaviour... In fact, there are many ways; you can only determine the one that's best for the individual by knowing her and understanding her autism. If your approach doesn't work, reflect on the reasons why and address these for the future.

Where we can go next

*   Beardon, L. and Worton, D. (eds) (2017) *Bittersweet on the Autism Spectrum.* London and Philadelphia, PA: Jessica Kingsley Publishers

    This book gathers together the thoughts and experiences of 28 individuals diagnosed on the autism spectrum. The topics are wide-ranging and offer insight into the challenges and celebrations that autism can bring.

* www.autismeducationtrust.org.uk

The Autism Education Trust (AET) is commissioned and funded by the Department for Education in England and partnered with three other organisations. The AET is dedicated to improving the education of children and young people on the spectrum and provides a wealth of resources focusing on education. These resources include access to the Inclusion Development Programmes, which were created in 2009, comprising interactive modules for professionals wanting to learn about autism in the early years, or in the primary and secondary years.

Chapter 3

PATHOLOGICAL DEMAND AVOIDANCE

3. The World on My String
(A poem about the characteristics of PDA)

I'm neurological with PDA
I love to dress up and make believe play.

Passive when young, dropping toys on the floor
I'm more active now than I was before.

Once delayed in my speech; I've learned to converse
Sometimes relaxed but sometimes the reverse.

Can mix with others but only when king
I'm powered up by the world on my string.

Anxious by nature, yet swiftly annoyed
Your social demands are mine to avoid.

If you want us to grow and to connect
Just let it be me who's always correct.

What we can learn

PDA stands for pathological demand avoidance and is now considered part of the autism spectrum, alongside autism and Asperger syndrome. The PDA profile was put forward by Elizabeth Newson in the 1980s and is therefore not a new and unknown condition. Curiously, however, it remains a poor relation when viewing the comparatively smaller body of research and literature, or when considering public awareness and understanding of the condition. Mention the words autism or Asperger syndrome to a stranger, for instance, and you can almost guarantee there will be a nod of recognition and accompanying anecdote that relates to someone's friend, a family member, a TV programme or film – but mention PDA and the response will probably be less exuberant and more hesitant. Even discussions among those who *are* familiar with the PDA profile are not generally straightforward, highlighting wide-ranging differences of opinion, for example, regarding both its occurrence as a separate condition and its label; some people prefer to use the word 'extreme' or 'rational' instead of 'pathological'.

My own interest in PDA has grown in the course of my work, alongside the increasing number of children presenting with such characteristics. Little by little, more and more, I find myself liaising with staff and parents who can describe autistic traits in their children but not attribute their successes to typical autism-friendly practices. These are the children who may thrive on change and novelty instead of routines and sameness. Children who can become the characters of their imagination and try to control people and situations in ways that suggest an unexpected degree of social awareness. Children whose anxieties form the bedrock of the condition and are so severe that they warrant the term 'pathological' – they will go to extreme lengths to avoid *any* kind of demands. Children who vary enormously from one to another, who will test the mettle of even the most skilled of adults and who ultimately lead us into previously uncharted territories of ingenuity.

How we can help

1. I often use the metaphor of a ladder with many rungs to explain how we can partition a skill into small, achievable steps. In the area of PDA, we could equate each rung to a target behaviour, where the lower rungs are those that must be dealt with first and the higher rungs are those that can be dealt with later. This idea of prioritising behaviours and essentially picking your battles is one that is commonly described in the literature on PDA. Refusing to wear socks and shoes is probably something you can accept for now, but hitting others is not, for example.

2. The Homunculi Approach may be suitable for children with PDA, as it is a cognitive behaviour therapy intervention designed for children on the spectrum and for people with emotional difficulties. It involves a child creating a series of gadgets and agents, which are used to address a particular mission (issue) in a pictorial way. The technique harnesses a child's creativity and is both structured and flexible. The approach is accredited to the authors Anne Greig and Tommy Mackay.

3. Children with PDA can find it hard to accept praise because this makes them feel that you are in charge, not them – that they have only done the work or task to please you. Don't be surprised by children who destroy something that you have just celebrated! Give praise indirectly and in a broader, general sense. And don't forget to look for those moments that are worth celebrating in the first place – recognise the things that

they are doing well, no matter how small (either to remind yourself that you are doing a good job or to ensure that your efforts are not solely focused on negative behaviours).

Where we can go next

* Christie, P., Duncan, M., Fidler, R. and Healy, Z. (2012) *Understanding Pathological Demand Avoidance Syndrome in Children*. London and Philadelphia, PA: Jessica Kingsley Publishers

  A comprehensive guide to PDA, which includes descriptions of the characteristic behaviours and relevant strategies, as well as information on how to develop children's emotional wellbeing.

* Greig, A. and Mackay, T. (2013) *The Homunculi Approach to Social and Emotional Wellbeing*. London and Philadelphia, PA: Jessica Kingsley Publishers

  This user-friendly book is designed for use with children aged 7 upwards and is self-contained, enabling a parent or practitioner to carry out the programme first-hand and without any prior knowledge. The authors explain the theory behind the approach and outline evidence of its success. A poster and photocopiable worksheets are included.

4. Mind your Pleas and Cues
(A poem about teaching strategies)

Don't mind if I don't. Don't mind if you do.
I don't know if I can. What about you?

I must insist on you doing and lending both hands.
It's my secret way of avoiding demands.

What's working today, may not on the next,
My focus is better when approaches are flexed.
Spontaneous decisions to seek compromise,
Make me look important and you look less wise.

Whenever I frustrate you, be an oasis of calm.
Harsh tones and high feelings will ring my alarms.
No easy feat, when we're mentally tired.
But neutral is best if you want what's required.

Consider the environment, the space where I learn,
So my anxiety is less along with sensory concern.
Let's make up a den or find a safe space
Somewhere I know I can recover with grace.

While swearing and rudeness is hard to ignore,
It's better than aggression and damage for sure.
Prioritise my needs with diplomacy and tact,
My behaviour improves when you do not react.

When making demands, leave room for manoeuvre,
Gauge my level of tolerance so responses are smoother.
Minimise, negotiate, change or reduce,
Tailor-make plans to my mood you've deduced.

Try to work with my changing interests
Use puppets and role play so I do not feel stressed.
Try out rewards but praise like I'm shy,
I will achieve lots but don't make me comply.

What we can learn

I seem to remember a television advert in the 1990s that referred to the credit card *Access* as being our flexible friend. It strikes me as a somewhat poignant metaphor for how we support children with PDA, since this generally involves endless and variable transactions (of patience and energy), fluctuating interest rates (managed by your creativity and enthusiasm) and a commitment to long-term repayments (acceptance that short-term gains will be small but eventually add up to something larger). Wryness aside, flexibility really should be a friend to your attitude and approach if you want to be an effective PDA practitioner or parent. In fact, flexibility is probably *the* most important tool you can own in your home/school toolbox. Being flexible means many things. It means you are ever ready to change the level of demands you make on your child so that this matches her level of tolerance at all times – reducing demands when you know she is anxious and increasing them when she seems more amenable. Flexibility is also crucial in terms of the strategies used. Conventional wisdom states that children on the spectrum are more responsive to consistency, using the same strategies and resources over and over. While this is partly true of children with PDA, my experience suggests that consistency and repetition are more effective for those with classical autism and Asperger syndrome than those with PDA. The nature of consistency and repetition in the PDA groups is perhaps more to do with being consistently and repeatedly *flexible*.

Our poem illustrates some of the practices currently advocated by many professionals in the field of PDA and I'd like to think that each verse is a lesson in flexibility. These lessons are not easy for adults to learn – letting go of the 'I'm the adult and you're the child who must do what I say' belief is an especially difficult lesson – but when learned are more likely to showcase your strengths as someone who is clear sighted, open minded, creative and resolute. Someone who is a *flexible friend*, helping children *access* and be included in their environment.

How we can help

1. Children with PDA typically thrive on novelty and may respond swiftly to a new resource or approach purely because it is new. However, they can be equally as swift in rejecting your resource or approach because the moment it starts to work is the moment the control passes to you! Don't assume that these can never be revisited in the future or that they can't be remodelled sooner.

2. One of the strategies that amuses me whenever I share it with training audiences is the one to do with health and safety policies. You can't escape health and safety measures in modern times but in this context they can be a definite boon. They can give the adult opportunity to sigh in mock exasperation and to admit that they are indeed a nuisance but also an explanation for some of the decisions that we 'unfortunately' have to make, for example blaming someone in authority for the fact that we have to line up to go outside or for the fact that we have to share equipment in class.

3. It is equally as important to recognise your own levels of tolerance as it is your child's. Just as we know we need to match our demands with the child's mood, so we need to match our mood with her demands. If we are not calm and relaxed then we are going to find it much more difficult if not impossible to implement any of the strategies suggested in the poem. Share the principles, techniques and resources that work best with at least one other adult, so that you are supported (rather than isolated) and can face each new challenge afresh.

Where we can go next

* Fidler, R. and Christie, P. (2015) *Can I Tell You about Pathological Demand Avoidance Syndrome?* London and Philadelphia, PA: Jessica Kingsley Publishers

  A short and helpful book explaining PDA through the eyes of an 11-year-old character called Issy. The book also contains practical advice on how to support individuals with PDA.

* The PDA Society (2016) *Pathological Demand Avoidance Syndrome. A Reference Booklet for Health, Education and Social Care Practitioners.* UK: The PDA Society. (Original work published in 2014.)

  A booklet introducing aspects of PDA, covering its history, key characteristics and comparisons with other conditions. It also includes a section written by Phil Christie, who explains how the condition may present in a child, and how practitioners and parents can help.

Chapter 4

WOMEN AND GIRLS

5. Acting Up
(A poem about masquerading)

Shining bright but they think I'm plain.
Standing so close, why can't they see
How my worries are secretly lain
Beneath performance and artistry?

Standing so close, why can't they see
It's their understanding I'm needing?
Beneath performance and artistry,
There's extreme effort in succeeding.

It's their understanding I'm needing.
Overloading is confused with quiet.
There's extreme effort in succeeding –
Quiet is codeword for RIOT.

Overloading is confused with quiet.
How my worries are secretly lain –
Quiet is codeword for riot.
Shining bright but they think I'm plain.

What we can learn

You might think that one of the defining characteristics of autism is a tendency to behave in the same way regardless of the company one is in, unaware that your behaviour is acceptable to some people but considered inappropriate by others (and subject to ridicule, embarrassment and disapproval). You might also think that people with autism have no social filter and carry on with glorious abandon, immune to other people's thoughts and feelings. But in this respect, you would be wrong. Many girls on the spectrum, for instance, have learned how to 'hide' some of their behaviours so that they don't stand out from their peers, copying what they see even if it makes them uncomfortable (e.g., pretending to have lots of friends, wearing the same clothes as their peers, going to parties). Others can have difficulties that are so subtle that their diagnosis would be perplexing to those regarding them with unknowing eyes. These are the girls who are often quiet, amenable and conscientious – the girls who don't get into trouble or create any problems, 'acting up' in the opposite sense of the phrase. While their performances may be convincing to the outside world, you can imagine that they put many girls at risk – not only in the situations they may inadvertently find themselves or in terms of their mental health, but also in the sense of their diagnosis being missed in the first place. 'Just because you can't you see it doesn't mean it's not there' – so says Sarah Hendrickx in the introduction to her book *Women and Girls with Autism Spectrum Disorder* (2015, p.15); surely a clarion call to improve awareness and understanding of how autism can present itself in females.

As I see it, the exploration of gender differences in autism is still a relatively new endeavour, though there are certainly many more books available now than there were in, say, the late 1990s when Donna Williams wrote *Somebody Somewhere* (1998). Today, we can look to adults such as Laura James, Cynthia Kim and

Liane Holliday Willey (who struggled in their earlier years with unrecognised difficulties) to read personal experiences of what it is like to be a female on the spectrum.

How we can help

1. Respect your daughter's need for space during or after social events, no matter how small, regular or trivial the event (having someone round for tea, visiting relatives, coming in from school or break, attending an appointment, being with friends, going out in town – these all require some degree of social effort). She might not look as if or realise she needs a break but she will probably feel much better for it afterwards.

2. Some girls may find it helpful to keep a diary or journal voicing worries and frustrations in private – allowing them to save face and let go at the same time. They can of course also be used to remember the funny, the outrageous and the successful moments of peer interactions…

3. I sometimes talk to families and staff about the risk of assuming that a highly verbal child will have an equally high level of understanding. The same could be said of a girl's social behaviour, that how she is acting is not necessarily indicative of social understanding – so be mindful of this.

Where we can go next

*   Hendrickx, S. (2015) *Women and Girls with Autism Spectrum Disorder*. London and Philadelphia, PA: Jessica Kingsley Publishers

    Sarah's book examines the presentation of autism in females and shows how it is different to that in males. Her exploration of topics across the age ranges shows that the subtleties of autism in females can present very real challenges – not only for the individuals masking their difficulties in order to fit in, but also in terms of others recognising and understanding their needs.

* Simone, R. (2010) *Aspergirls*. London and Philadelphia, PA: Jessica Kingsley Publishers

Rudy has coined the term *Aspergirls* to describe females who have been diagnosed with Asperger syndrome. Her book captures the voices of many Aspergirls, expressing their thoughts and feelings relating to a wide range of topics in daily life, such as school, sensory overload, puberty, depression and old age. Each chapter concludes with advice for Aspergirls and their parents.

6. Tried and Tested

(A poem about unmasking)

Autism denied earns me a badge
Without pride.
To mask is to hide.

Losing my disguise brings disbelief and
Surprise.
Yet means no more lies.

What we can learn

I expect you are familiar with the phrase 'everyone has a role to play', but I wonder what it means to you. It might mean how you work within a team. It might refer to your stance on a topical issue. Or it might mean how you act in a certain situation, assuming a specific code of conduct. How one behaves at work or school, for instance, is usually different to how one behaves at home. Such differences are frequently noted with autistic children, often in terms of their demeanour, skills and level of compliance, for example being calm and cooperative in one place but not in another.

We also have lots of instances where autistic behaviours are pronounced unequally between settings – where children mask their difficulties or that these are more subtle according to the context. I have witnessed this myself on many occasions, seeing the same child act in one way with parents but another way with staff in school. I have also experienced this during home–school discussions, where parents or staff describe strengths or needs that contrast with those described by their counterparts. It can sometimes come as quite a shock to adults to find that children who present as able in one setting are significantly affected by their autism elsewhere – or even, that the person has a diagnosis in the first place. The girl in our poem provides us with an apposite example through her disclosure – deciding to reveal her autism, to *un*mask and to assume her 'natural' role (rather than her 'fitting in' role). Being open about the diagnosis brings relief but prompts suspicion from peers because they have never seen her act like this before. Perhaps they are wondering why she now has autism or why is she acting 'more autistically'. What they have not yet realised is that her admission frees her to be true to herself at last.

How we can help

1. If your child wants to disclose her autism diagnosis, take some time to think about who needs to know and how this will be shared. She may assume that it is important to tell

everyone and to provide as much detail as possible. However, her version of 'everyone' may be different from yours (strangers in the street, people in public, all of the children in her year group etc.). She will need guidance to ensure that the disclosure promotes understanding and support, rather than confusion and embarrassment – or worse.

2. As the young person comes to terms with her diagnosis, there may be times where she feels that autism is a justification for behaving in certain ways, failing to see why she should change her behaviour. In such instances, you may need to teach her that the name is an explanation for some of her thoughts, feelings and behaviours but not the sum of them. She need not believe that autism precludes her ability to cope with situations that are 'expected' to be hard for people on the spectrum.

3. For those who want to find out more about their diagnosis, be aware of the information they are referencing and offer reputable sources. You don't need to exhaust discussions on the person's diagnosis – be guided by their level of interest – but it is important to know what they are basing their thoughts and feelings on.

Where we can go next

* Frenz, F. (2013) *How to be Human*. Berkeley, CA: Creston Books

Florida's book is geared towards primary and early secondary aged children, helping them understand autism through the eyes of a teenage girl. The text is candid and accompanied by colourful illustrations. Her writing includes consideration of how we can choose to be who we are.

* Holliday Willey, L. (2004) *Pretending to be Normal*. London and New York, NY: Jessica Kingsley Publishers. (Original work published in 1999.)

Liane talks about her life and family as a person with Asperger syndrome, reflecting on the past and present. There are seven appendices offering further advice and support for others on the spectrum. The first appendix is called *Explaining Who You Are to Those Who Care* (p.97) and focuses on the pros and cons of disclosing a diagnosis.

Chapter 5

SENSORY PROCESSING

7. Whatdoido?

(A poem about sensory systems)

Ohh! What do I do with my feet?

These strangers that lead me and never retreat.

Ohh! What do I do with my legs?
These beings that hang

like   from

    washing   pegs.

Ohh! What do I do with my hands?
These drifters that
        shadow
          me
around aLieN lands.

Ohh! What do I do with my arms?
These outsiders that remind me
   of
  wind
milling
 farms.

Ohh! What do I do with my head?
This intruder that butts into
thethingsthataresaid.

Ohh! What of this body I'm in?
                    e
This unsteerable vess
                l
that's powered by stim.

St u tt er ing and starting
When <u>heavy</u> with load.
Too many demands
                    will sign it
                        off
                            r
                                o
                                    a
                                        d.

What we can learn

In the introduction to Naoki Higashida's (2013) book *The Reason I Jump*, David Mitchell paints an emphatic picture of sensory anguish. He helps us imagine what it would be like to be a person whose sensory systems are not working properly – where everything heard, seen, smelt or felt is unregulated, uncoordinated and turned up high. Where sensory (di)stress is further intensified by the inability to communicate the problem and the inability to regain control over oneself. David suggests that such experiences occurring on a regular basis in people without autism would likely drive them to the brink – less able to manage something that is a recurring reality for many on the spectrum. We are not talking about a general dislike of Marmite here. Nor a tendency to wince at scraping nails. We are potentially talking about stop-you-in-your-tracks-and-shut-you-down, fight and flight responses. These are responses that render the person incapable of carrying on in the moment until sensory order is resumed.

We shall look at a number of sensory challenges throughout the book, exploring how they affect children in different ways in different situations. For now, we can refer to our poem above and take with us an example of a child who is struggling with two hitherto 'unknown' sensory systems – the proprioceptive and vestibular systems. These are the systems that increasingly crop up in my discussions with parents and professionals and the ones that people are less familiar with initially. The proprioceptive system provides children with a map of their body, helping them know where their limbs are in relation to themselves in physical space and to grade their movements with appropriate pressure. This system may reveal itself in children who tire more quickly than others, who have difficulty dressing, like pressing onto things, struggle with handwriting, squeeze into tight spaces, are clumsy, light- or heavy-handed, and have issues judging personal space or negotiating obstacles. The vestibular system is associated with speed, direction, orientation, balance and movement. Behaviours that you may observe in this area are likely to include spinning and twirling, running rather than walking, hanging upside down, walking around the edges of open spaces, difficulty with stairs, or a need to be off the ground.

The child in our poem is someone beset by the problem of coordinating and moving parts of her body because the messages being sent from her brain are jumbled and bunching up like cars in a traffic jam. The more she tries to control her body, the more difficult it becomes – and the more likely she will 'crash'.

How we can help

1. Many of you will be familiar with the idea of a 'sensory diet'. A diet of food is healthy when it involves eating the right food in the right amounts at regular intervals. If we eat the wrong food or too much of it, we feel unwell. If we only eat once a day, the benefits are temporary and we probably spend the rest of the time craving food – to the detriment of our concentration on everything else. A *sensory* diet works in the same way, in that it is most effective with regular nourishment (not once a day), with an appropriate blend of activities (for the relevant sensory system/s) and the right level of intensity (alerting or calming).

2. Many of the sensory diets I read begin life as a report with invaluable advice and ideas presented as pictures or under particular headings. However, you can't make a cake from a list of ingredients, so to speak. If you have been provided with lots of activities, choose a (balanced) handful and then decide when and where they will be done, and how long you will spend on them. Don't try to do them all at once. Your plan should not be complicated or excessively detailed but might state times, places and who is going to do them. Something as simple as a list on your fridge, a timetable on your classroom wall or a laminated copy of the activities (marked through the day) may suffice.

3. While you may be confident that the activities are going to help your child, she may be more wary, resistant or avoidant. Try to think of these as typical autistic responses, for what you are introducing is likely to be new or different. We don't want to force children into sensory activities (they should be enjoyable) but we can have faith and be persistent. Just because she didn't like the vibrating pillow, the blanket wrap

or the chewy chew the first time, doesn't mean she won't like it in the future.

Where we can go next

* Bogdashina, O. (2016) *Sensory Perceptual Issues in Autism and Asperger Syndrome*. London and Philadelphia, PA: Jessica Kingsley Publishers. (Original work published in 2003.)

An informative book that discusses sensory processing difficulties in the context of sensory experiences, perceptual styles and cognition. Possible interventions are provided and an assessment sheet for drawing up a sensory profile is included.

* Laurie, C. (2014) *Sensory Strategies*. London: The National Autistic Society

Geared towards professionals working in education, this book provides information about the different sensory systems and suggests ideas for managing difficulties.

8. Long Sleeves
(A poem about clothing)

It's
Very
Hard for me
To wear long sleeves
Over my elbows or below my knees.
They press down on my skin and make me wheeze.
The more clothes I
Wear the more
I will
Freeze.

What we can learn

If you have watched the 1999 movie *The World is Not Enough*, you will have seen the scene where the characters James Bond and Elektra King are chased across the snow and become part of an avalanche that sends them crashing down the mountain. Saved by a circular inflatable that wraps itself around them, Elektra panics in the darkness and James has to slice through the material to force their release. Why do I use this preamble? Because this feeling of claustrophobia and entrapment is possibly something close to that experienced by children with a sensory aversion to sleeves, coats, socks, shoes or clothing in general. Over the years, I have met many children who hate wearing coats or tops with long sleeves and refuse to put them on whatever the weather. I've also come across children who wear their coat at half mast around their elbows, children who cast their coat aside whenever they get the opportunity, and children whose shoes seem to have the power of ejection. Of course, these habits are not unusual in the grand scheme but the motivations are probably different for children with autism. For some, the intolerance may be an issue of material rubbing against their skin – perhaps the slip-sliding movement across their body when they move is very irritating or creates a rustling noise that is distracting. Some children may not like the material because it feels too tickly and cope better when it is denser and heavier. Other children may refuse to wear a coat or sleeves because they don't register the fact that they are cold (or take longer to feel cold) and don't automatically associate cold temperatures with the need for warm clothing.

How we can help

1. You could put a weather board by the outside door to show children what the conditions are like outside (being technical for those who like details and facts) and what clothing is needed. This will at least explain the reason for wearing a coat when it is cold or a hat when it is sunny and – as a year-round practice – might reduce some of the confrontations. It will also mean that you can give children a warning and show them what they need *before* they go outside, not *after* they have rushed through the door and you are 'interrupting' their play to march them back indoors…

2. Think about the textures and materials that your child can tolerate, or tolerates more. Body warmers might be an option since these provide warmth without covering up arms. Or layer up with cotton jumpers and loose-fitting sleeves if children can cope with soft cotton. Alternatively, you may find that some children are more accepting of sleeves and clothing when these are harder to remove and more snug to the skin; once children know that the clothes cannot be removed, they can shift their attention to something else.

This principle extends to footwear too. Shoes that are easy to slip off are going to be slipped off. Heavier footwear will help children feel more anchored and be harder to remove. Where children insist on removing their footwear in school, you could have a special box to put the shoes in and try slipper socks.

3. If you find that no amount of preparation or experimenting with types of coats, fastenings and footwear seems to be working, then you may need to opt for the 'all in' tactic (and some of you may prefer to do this from the outset anyway). By all in, I mean deciding that the child has to wear her coat whether she wants to or not because this is in the best interests of her health and wellbeing: if we use the argument that we wouldn't let a child go outside without any clothes on, despite her protests, then we could ask ourselves why this rule shouldn't extend to coats in cold weather. Your 'insistence', however, would still be managed in a way that respects her sensory difficulties, for example building up the time she is expected to wear the coat.

Where we can go next

* Kim, C. (2014) *Nerdy, Shy, and Socially Inappropriate*. London and Philadelphia, PA: Jessica Kingsley Publishers

Chapter 10 illustrates ways in which higher order thinking affects our ability to plan, make decisions, inhibit responses and prioritise actions. It also describes the nature of interoception – the body's sensitivity to sensations relating to, for example, breathlessness, hunger, thirst, temperature and pain. Cynthia explains how to 'jumpstart the process' (p.172).

❋ Smith Myles, B., Tapscott Cook, K., Miller, N.E., Rinner, L. and Robbins, L.A. (2000) *Asperger Syndrome and Sensory Issues*. Shawnee, KS: Autism Asperger Publishing Company (AAPC)

Chapter 4 suggests a number of interventions that can be used to help individuals with sensory processing difficulties. There are checklists and questions to consider when gathering information, as well as grids stating possible problems and potential solutions.

9. Take Care (Labels)
(A poem about labels)

> *Labels*
> *Restricting, insensitive*
> *Itching, scratching, grating*
> *Discomfort burning and radiating*
> *Brands.*

What we can learn

We have already seen that children can have issues wearing clothes and sleeves due to their sensitivity to touch. Sometimes, however, it is not the article of clothing itself or the material that is the main concern, but a particular part of it. Seams, stitching, cuffs, buttons, zips, loose threads, labels and hanging loops – these can all pose different problems for different children. They are either completely fascinating (on their own clothes or on others'), or extremely distracting, prompting children to repeatedly attempt to remove the offending part, chew on it, or undo it. This poem, for instance, concerns a child who cannot bear the feel of labels in her clothing and, presumably, cannot function or concentrate until these are cut away.

How we can help

1. If labels are causing repeated irritation then the easiest way to help is to remove them from the clothing. Remember, however, that children who are very sensitive to touch will notice if you have left the stub, so make sure it is removed completely. Some children may need to see you removing the label or need to see the label after it is removed to trust that the item won't cause further irritation: just telling them you have done it might not be enough when it comes to getting dressed.

2. Try setting up a box of labels that the child can explore if she is intensely distracted by them on her clothing. Alternatively, you could provide her with a container of colourful ribbon varying in texture and width, which she could customise to make her own labels.

3. For children who are preoccupied with threads and seams in their socks or cuffs, you could provide them with an alternative such as a ball of wool or a bag of variable strings. What you might also want to consider, however, is when this behaviour presents itself most often, as it could be a stimulatory behaviour driven by 'boredom' or stress. In such instances, the trigger might not be related to sensory sensitivities (e.g., an irritating thread) but to a lack of structure or confusing demands.

Where we can go next

* Marks & Spencer (2018) *Easy Dressing School Uniform.* Accessed on 02/02/2018 at www.marksandspencer.com/l/ kids/school-uniform/easy-dressing-school-uniform/easy-dressing-school-uniform-range

  Autism-friendly or 'Easy Dressing' clothing is now part of the company's merchandise and has been developed in association with The National Autistic Society. A range of school garments is available for ages 2–16. Check out the reviews and items for yourself to see if they would be suitable for your child.

* www.sensorysmart.co.uk

  An online company offering, among other products, seamless and seamfree clothing for children.

Chapter 6

SOCIAL INTERACTIONS

10. The Invisible Switch
(A poem about difficulties with eye contact)

I have in my head an invisible switch
Which
Mostly works but has the occasional glitch.

The switch is my prompt to look up from the floor
Before
I respond to your words and add something more.

When the switch malfunctions you will not know why
I
Am unable to gaze straight into your eye.

Anxiety which surges through my fuse box
Knocks
Out the switch resisting your eye contact shocks.

What we can learn

In 2002, an article was published in an American journal, concluding that social competence in people with autism could be predicted by the way that they looked at others in a social situation (Klin *et al.* 2002). The participants in the study were fitted with an eye tracking device and tasked with watching five clips from the (1966) film *Who's Afraid of Virginia Woolf?*, directed by Mike Nichols. The results compared the responses of 15 autistic males with a control group and revealed that those with autism were more likely to look at the actors' mouths than their eyes. Inspired by my recollection of this experiment, I decided to run a quick check on the internet to draw comparisons with other studies – and soon found one emphasising the impact of *language*. In this instance, researchers claimed that the viewing behaviour of people with autism would differ according to how competent they were with language. Somewhat surprisingly, their findings indicated that the more proficient speakers would focus on the actors' mouths when watching a social scene more than those with weaker language skills (Norbury *et al.* 2009).

Together, these studies propose that appropriate eye gaze is linked to social competence but not necessarily guaranteed with better language skills. It's a fascinating topic and obviously still an area very much of interest to researchers, given the abundance of other experiments trying to understand how and why eye gaze can be different or difficult for people on the spectrum. When I am talking to another person I know that I should make eye contact but find it very uncomfortable. Eye contact, for me, is a painful and mechanical process, something I have to consciously think about every time I am with someone, following instructions delivered by an unknown voice in my head at regular intervals.

How we can help

1. Where you position yourself when talking to an individual may go some way towards helping her feel more comfortable with you – so try sitting or standing beside her, or sitting at

an angle. This should make it feel less confrontational or overwhelming.

2. The person may also feel more comfortable if she has a prop to hold or use during the interaction, such as a pencil and paper for notes or doodles (e.g., during a table activity or a meal out) or a pocket-sized fidget object (e.g., for playtimes or when meeting visitors).

3. If you know that the individual struggles with social interactions and close proximity with others during conversations, then be proactive not only in supporting her during the moment, but also in helping her regulate anxieties – preceding 'stressful' situations with something relaxing and then offering time and space to recharge afterwards.

Where we can go next

* Bogdashina, O. (2010) *Autism and the Edges of the Known World*. London and Philadelphia, PA: Jessica Kingsley Publishers

Chapter 7 explores different aspects of non-verbal communication and how these may present in people with autism.

* Chown, N. (2017) *Understanding and Evaluating Autism Theory*. London and Philadelphia, PA: Jessica Kingsley Publishers

The final chapter in this instructive book is called 'What has 70 years taught us about autism?' and tackles some interesting questions. There is a short comment on the relevance of eye contact.

11. Eyes' Sight
(A poem about using eye contact)

There are windows with colour
On the left and the right
Spots shrink or get fuller
They change with the light.

On the left and the right
There are shutters with fringes
They change with the light
Both move on top hinges.

There are shutters with fringes
Closing at night
Both move on top hinges
Opening at first light.

Closing at night
Spots shrink or get fuller
Opening at first light
There are windows with colour.

What we can learn

Try as I might, I have never been able to make sense of a magic eye picture. In the past, I have crossed my eyes and looked at an upturned index finger for so long that it's given me a headache or made me queasy, but still not seen the image so tantalisingly hidden. Perhaps it would help if I knew what I was looking for or if there was an indication of where the image was situated; a clue would make it much easier. Until then, it's a classic case of looking but not seeing. In wider spheres, Peter Vermeulen's book *Autism as Context Blindness* (2012) provides us with a precise picture of how people on the spectrum need clues and specific prompts to make sense of information so that they can react or respond in appropriate ways. The context is vital. When we understand this, we can make reasonable inferences and deductions that help us know how to behave. When people are having a conversation, for instance, it is conventional to make eye contact but not to stare and study the different elements making up the eyes (like the person in our poem). The scrutiny would be more relevant, however, if the person had something in her eye or she was talking to an ophthalmologist. Children with autism find it hard to identify and process the most important details in a scene or situation and won't intuitively realise that the salient details can fluctuate. Consider, for example, trying to understand whether a person with tears in her eyes is happy, worried or distressed. Clearly, it isn't just about 'wet' eyes – there are many other factors to take into consideration. Inferences and deductions are notoriously tricky for children who are orientated to details and literal in their interpretations, basing their responses on singular pieces of information. I only go to bed when it is dark. People who smile at me are my friends. A person who bumps into me is a bully. We always drive this way to the park. I have to put my hand up when I want to say something. While these conclusions could be true in one context, they could equally be very wide of the mark in another.

How we can help

1. In Peter Vermeulen's book, he gives us the idea of 'pushing the context button' (p.360), which I have interpreted as highlighting the most important information for individuals to think about in a social situation – giving children clues and strategies to use. If we remind children that it is polite to say hello to someone who greets us, then they have a better

mode of response when the person approaches (e.g., rather than absconding or trying to climb on them).

2. Contextual differences mean that skills learned in one environment may warrant adaptation in another. We can put our hand up to ask a question in a group discussion, but would not do this if the adult was beside us one to one or we were with our family. When we learn to clean our hands, we should be able to complete the sequence whether the taps are pressed, lifted or automated and whether there is a towel, dispenser or hand dryer. Children may need to be taught how to practise and apply their learning in a range of situations rather than just one.

3. Graphic organisers are devices that give written information visual structure – highlighting the most relevant parts, making it easier to understand. They are, therefore, handy when working on paper-based exercises, such as homework or classwork, because they give children strong visual clues as to what details are required, when and where. Graphic organisers can include thought clouds to generate ideas, boxes to show children where to put their work, and spaces to show how many words are required in an answer. Tasks may also be numbered to encourage a logical order, or colour coded, underlined, emphasised in bold type or marked with arrows and bullets.

Where we can go next

* Vermeulen, P. (2012) *Autism as Context Blindness*. Shawnee, KS: Autism Asperger Publishing Company. (Original work published in 2009.)

Chapter 2 explains the role of the brain in understanding context and shows why people with autism may notice some details that others would not, and suggests how this can be an advantage or problematic when interpreting information in everyday life. The final chapter shows us how we can apply an understanding of 'context blindness' to strategies and interventions.

* www.stephenwiltshire.co.uk

Stephen is a gifted artist, able to produce detailed panoramic drawings of cities he has seen (only briefly) from the air. He is regularly commissioned for artwork representing places around the world and he has a gallery in London. This website showcases some of his work, highlights projects past and present, and features video clips of Stephen drawing.

12. Intensive Interaction
(A poem about intensive interaction)

(Child's voice and then *the adult's*)

duh
– duh

dee ee
– dee ee

guh duh gee
– guh duh gee

guh-duh guh-duh
– guh-duh guh-duh

duga duga duga-duga-duga
– duga duga duga-duga-duga.

What we can learn

It has been said that 'If a child cannot learn in the way we teach, we must teach in a way the child can learn' (The Lovaas Institute n.d.). I've come across this quote on various occasions but only recently discovered that the author was referring to children with autism – and that its origins are roughly located in the same time period that 'intensive interaction' was conceived. The practice of intensive interaction has grown in stature since the late 1980s, and was developed by Dave Hewett and Melanie Nind as a means of engaging with children and adolescents attending a school on the site of a long-stay London hospital (Hewett 2017). Phoebe Caldwell also champions this approach and has written a number of books on the subject.

The approach is often used with individuals who are pre-verbal and 'hard to reach' – individuals yet to acquire the fundamental skills and motivations needed to interact and communicate with others. In its simplest form, intensive interaction means being available for an interaction with the child, watching her behaviour and then responding. This can involve the adult echoing her sounds, imitating her gestures or copying her movements. To the casual observer, it may look as if the child is the lead performer and the adult the appreciative audience – inviting questions as to what and how she is learning. The questions are not unreasonable. The adult is after all led by the child and reacts enthusiastically during the show of behaviour. However, adults well versed in the approach know that it is not about scanning the child to make a social photocopy. In fact, the adult is subtly introducing elements of turn-taking and reciprocity in communication. When the child makes a sound, the adult pauses and repeats the sound – looking to see if she notices before making the sound again. When appropriate, the adult can then provide variations and alternatives during interactions to move them on. This promotes the idea of back and forth exchanges and demonstrates that these are interesting, useful and enjoyable.

How we can help

1. Above all, enjoy it! Intensive interaction may feel more instinctive and natural with very young children but stranger with those who are older. It's important, however, to recognise the developmental level of children as well as their chronological age. The freer you are to join in with their sounds, movements and mannerisms, the more successes you are likely to have.

2. Children will respond better when adults respect the ideas of 'quality not quantity' and 'less is more'. An individual session may be as brief as a few seconds but then be repeated on one or more occasions, building up the time incrementally and as appropriate. Remember that you will be trying to demonstrate the enjoyment of interaction with someone who has not yet learned this and whose attention span is probably short.

3. When you are beginning to use intensive interaction, think about what the child can do already and thus what you expect as realistic goals. Be clear about the communication signals you will look for (e.g., making eye contact, anticipating your sound echo or moving closer to you) so that you can equally be clear about the progress being made.

Where we can go next

* Caldwell, P. and Horwood, J. (2008) *Using Intensive Interaction and Sensory Integration.* London and Philadelphia, PA: Jessica Kingsley Publishers

The authors show how intensive interaction strategies combined with an understanding of sensory processing can be used to support children (and adults) on the spectrum who may be pre-verbal, have a significant learning disability and who present 'behavioural distress' (p.7).

* www.intensiveinteraction.org

An invaluable source for learning more about the approach, including its history, key principles, core techniques, useful resources and training. There are also video demonstrations available via links with YouTube.

Chapter 7

MANAGING EMOTIONS

13. A Moment with Alexi Thymia
(A poem about alexithymia)

If you are upset
And I do not help you
Don't think I don't care
Because that's wholly untrue.

The emotions you're feeling
I feel even stronger
So my processing time
Takes that little bit longer.

During the moment
When I'm staring at you
I'm wrestling with choices
As to the right thing to do.

The confusion of feelings
Makes me stiffen and freeze
– not the indifference
The external world sees.

So whenever there's a problem
Or you feel full of woe
Remember I care more than
You are likely to know.

What we can learn

Having read Daniel Tammet's book *Embracing the Wide Sky* (2009), I am drawn to his idea of questioning the link between intelligence and intelligent behaviour. It makes me wonder about the relationship between emotional intelligence and the intelligence of emotional responses. In other words, can we judge the emotional capacity of a person purely on the basis of how they respond to someone in a moment – assuming that the person who doesn't do or say the *right* thing doesn't care? Surely we can't. First, emotional responses of and from a person are uniquely subjective. What one person views as sad news may be regarded as shocking by another – and who is to say what the correct response is in any situation? Second, a person's current emotional state may interfere with their capacity to empathise with the other person. It might be hard, for example, to celebrate someone's good fortune when you are personally feeling stressed or upset. Also, every one of us varies according to our life experiences and therefore the experiences we have had of different (emotionally charged) situations.

So…what does this mean for the child who laughs when someone is nervous? The teenager who breezes past his crying sister? Or the daughter who insists on the attention of her sleep-deprived mother? Do these seemingly absent, unsympathetic or misplaced feelings mean that children with autism don't care about others? In essence, no. It is true that individuals struggle with emotions but it is not true that they lack them or that they are unable to empathise. Notwithstanding their cognitive ability, age and verbal skills, they just might not show it in the expected way (yet to learn). They may not realise that a response is needed (*miss*-interpreting the emotion) or they may fail to show it at the appropriate moment (putting their own needs first). In addition to this, we know that children with autism *can* be sensitive, thoughtful and caring but do not always have the words or actions in their vocabulary to express what they feel (like the girl in the poem). This particular phenomenon, incidentally, has a name: alexithymia.

How we can help

1. Children with autism can learn new skills when we *model* what to do and give them opportunity to practise. Where possible and practical, situations that the young person struggled with should be revisited afterwards so that she knows why the other person was angry, upset, worried and so on, and can be given ways to help next time.

2. Stories are a great way to explore emotions and feelings with young children and discussion around characters can help adults determine their level of understanding and the thought processes behind this. For example, if the story portrays an upset child, how does the young person (with autism) perceive the character's emotion? Can she identify the reasons for the emotion and what would she have done in response?

3. You could teach children how to understand and respond to emotionally charged situations by starting with representations of these in pictures (which are easily located on the internet). By inviting children to describe what they see, you can show them what the most important elements of the scene are and thus teach them what to do and what to say. These phrases and behaviours can be rehearsed in role play.

Where we can go next

* Kim, C. (2015) *Nerdy, Shy, and Socially Inappropriate*. London and Philadelphia, PA: Jessica Kingsley Publishers

  In Chapter 9, entitled 'Exploring the Emotional Landscape', Cynthia discusses some of the difficulties she has when articulating emotions. She offers strategies for supporting someone who has alexithymia.

* www.positivepenguins.com

  A website that links to an app called *Positive Penguins*. The app allows primary-aged children to explore different emotions in a personal way, writing about an emotional trigger and learning ways of managing this through successive 'story' pages.

14. Green and Happy Feet
(A poem about emotion thermometers)
(Verses should be read from left to right)

I have got a useful chart

A handy memory aid

When the pressure builds inside

It helps bad feelings fade

Emotion red is at the top

Very bright and vivid

When I say I'm at a five

It means I'm so so livid

At this point I leave the room

And go out for a walk

I find my den and snuggle in

This is not the time to talk.

Emotion orange is one below

As shiny as paint gloss

When I say I'm at a four

You will know I'm cross

At this point I take a break

Breathing in and out

I'll keep my hands deep in my pockets

And think how not to shout.

Emotion blue is in the middle

The one that's often stated

When I say I'm at a three

I'm sorely irritated

At this point I need my ball

To squeeze out bits of stress

I'll try to say what's on my mind

So you don't have to guess.

Emotion yellow is underneath

It's almost Korma curried

When I say I'm at a two

It means I'm rather worried

At this point I need a friend

To make me feel secure

Remind me of my strengths and talents

And squash those doubts once more.

Emotion green is first and best

Green like leaves of palm

When I say I'm at a one

I know I'm nice and calm

At this point my heart is even

Steady in its beat

I can focus on my work

And tap my happy feet.

What we can learn

Professor Steve Peters is a consultant psychiatrist and the author of *The Chimp Paradox* (2012), a book that has been endorsed by sportsmen and women for its impact on their performance and successes. Throughout the book, the author shows how our behaviour is influenced by our thoughts and feelings, illustrating the difference between logical and emotional approaches to situations, and referring to these as 'shades' first and 'black and whites' second. It reminds me of the ways in which children with autism can view the world and respond to different triggers, be they fixed or fluid, obvious or invisible, significant or trivial. Children's interpretations and reactions are influenced by many factors but especially according to how emotive the situation is or how emotional they are feeling. Many parents and staff, for example, can talk about children who are generally passive and amenable, while others can talk about children whose reactions are rapid and more intense – happy and relaxed in one moment but upset and raging in the next. If it's difficult for adults to spot the warning signs, imagine how difficult it is for children (especially if stresses accumulate silently throughout the day). Emotional regulation is one of many recurring themes in my book – something that children find hard to understand and apply. How can you have control over your emotions if your thinking style affects your interpretation of something you can see or feel, and affects your ability to recognise and communicate the problem? There isn't an easy answer unfortunately, but we know that visual structures are often helpful, teaching individuals how to recognise and deal with emotions in more rational ways. This poem introduces us to one such tool, which is called an emotion thermometer (or scale).

How we can help

1. Visual scales are tremendously versatile and can be applied to all manner of situations, showing children how a situation, thought, emotion or behaviour can have more than two options. Volume scales can denote levels of speaking; emotion scales can cover shades of feelings; and behaviour scales can clarify degrees of appropriate, inappropriate and dangerous behaviour.

2. Ensure that the options identified by the thermometer are available when they are needed (i.e., do not remain lost, incomplete, inoperable or distant). This will help the person trust in the measures that have been determined, help her be proactive in seeking and using them, and help you establish whether they are consistently effective.

3. Allow time for the person to learn how to use the thermometer and practise using it across the full range of emotions, not only in times of 'crisis', building a positive association with the tool (learning how to use it when calm) and demonstrating the breadth of emotions (making the tool dynamic). Review its effectiveness on a regular basis so that strategies are kept up to date.

Where we can go next

* Dunn Buron, K. and Curtis, M. (2004) *The Incredible 5-Point Scale*. Shawnee, KS: Autism Asperger Publishing Company. (Original work published in 2003.)

This book contains lots of photocopiable resources relating to a range of social situations. The authors have also contributed to the development of an app called *Autism Help!* which provides the user with a customisable electronic version of the 5-Point Scale. The app is produced by the Autism Society of Minnesota, AuSM®, and funded by the Minnesota Department of Human Service.

* Ross, T. (2017) *My Book of Feelings*. London and Philadelphia, PA: Jessica Kingsley Publishers

A picture book useful for explaining different feelings to primary-aged children.

Chapter 8

WELLBEING AND MENTAL HEALTH

15. Can't Sleep Won't Sleep
(A poem about worries and anxieties)

Alone in my bed
Ruminating on worries
Blooming in my head.

Panic throws its seeds
Seeds flower in the darkness
Unwelcome like weeds.

Sleep's out, now fallow.
Overshadowed by sunrise
Thoughts wither, sallow.

What we can learn

As I write this, I am trying to ignore my cold and the distracting possibility that germs have things in common with worries. Both are invisible to the naked eye and can multiply rapidly. Both reveal a whole host of nasties once 'under the microscope' and both are hard to eradicate completely. Maybe I should have used the idea of germs in my poem... As it happens, my inspiration came from a lexically similar word – that of *germ*ination, showing how a worry can spring into existence, take root and flourish under the 'wrong' conditions. Here we have a seed that grows strong in the dark but weakens in the light. When the individual goes to bed and all is quiet, she is finally left alone with the multitude of thoughts, feelings and experiences that have accumulated during the day and, most likely, focuses on the ones that carry more emotional weight: the fears, anxieties and worries. The more she thinks about these, the more they grow and the more difficult it is to sleep.

Worries and anxieties are known in us all but have a special significance for people with autism. In the first instance, what a child with autism deems a worry may seem surprising, trivial, extreme or irrational to others (i.e., the things that worry them would not prompt anxiety in others or present to the same degree). Examples could include worry of doors opening, stories ending unhappily, people moving their toys out of line, 'everyone' looking at them, food touching, noise or being late. Children may also hold onto their worries longer than you would expect – and long after the problem has been dealt with (persisting in a thought habit). In other contexts, children may become so consumed by their worries that these affect increasingly more aspects of daily life, for example a worry about pigeons in the local park becomes a worry about seeing any bird anywhere. Some worries won't necessarily be unusual but will still be problematic. What if the child is unable to communicate and share the worry (perhaps struggling with the language needed or expecting the adult to know without being told)? What if the child does not understand the feelings she has when the worry presents itself (misinterpreting butterflies in her tummy, shaking hands or faster heart rate)? And what if the child has a persistently negative take on life and assumes she is always right (unable to accept a counter argument or piece of advice)? Worries are difficult things to broach with children; our support will be more valuable if we respect the worries and avoid platitudes like 'There's nothing to worry about.' At best, the literal nature of this statement will upset children and at worst it will encourage them to retreat further inwards, believing that no one is able to understand them.

How we can help

1. Certain conditions are likely to make worries ripe for the picking though these will vary from one person to another. Try to establish whether there is a pattern of *when* the worries develop (e.g., Sunday night before school, when she is on her own, among a crowd, once she has gone to bed) so that you can both be proactive in preventing them. More structure and practical activities may help in some instances (keeping busy), while changes in the environment may be helpful in others (keeping calm).

2. You know yourself that it is hard to stop thinking about a worry because the effort required to resist something is greater than the effort required to accept it. Children might find it easier to cope, therefore, if they can learn what I would call a 'thought script' – a series of words, phrases or sentences that they should use whenever a worry starts to bloom. These words, phrases or sentences will essentially be positive thoughts that make the person feel happy (e.g., a favourite colour, a preferred toy, a favourite song, a personal mantra).

3. Some children may find it helpful to list or draw their worries, for eample in a special notebook, on sticky notes, on paper or on a whiteboard. These worries could be shared with a trusting adult to consider solutions or to be symbolically

removed: paper worries can be made into aeroplanes and thrown away; they can be posted into a worry monster and eaten; or they can be torn up and shredded.

Where we can go next

* Collins-Donnelly, K. (2013) *Starving the Anxiety Gremlin.* London and Philadelphia, PA: Jessica Kingsley Publishers

Kate's book is a workbook geared towards children aged 10 and above. The activities are grounded in principles of cognitive behaviour therapy and can be used by the individual in private study, or alongside a parent or professional.

* Hartman, D. (2017) *Beating Anxiety*. London and Philadelphia, PA: Jessica Kingsley Publishers

A concise guide to anxiety, this book would be suitable for teenagers or children at the latter end of their primary school years. Children can use it like a manual, learning to recognise, understand and manage their anxiety.

16. Long Haul Plight
(A poem about depression)

My mind is travelling
on a long haul
flight.
The end is unknown
not nearly in sight.

My shutters are drawn and prevent any light.
The darkness inside is
blacker than
night.

What we can learn

If you know someone who suffers with depression or if you suffer with it yourself, you will know that it is a terrible thing. It is like an invisible weight that you carry with you wherever you go whatever you are doing, yet at the same time, seem unable to see or grasp or shift. Just how do you tackle a force that is simultaneously concealed within the mind and so pervasive that it turns the person inside out and upside down, transforming them into someone unrecognisable by the way that they think, talk and behave? One of the things I have noticed during my career is the way in which conversations about depression can be diluted by people favouring the more generic label of 'mental health'. While this may be appropriate in circumstances where no specific clinical diagnosis has been made or people are respecting privacy, I think it also runs the risk of trivialising a condition that can have devastating consequences when inadequately treated.

Especially for people on the spectrum. Attwood and Garnett (2016) suggest that 35 per cent or more of adults with Asperger syndrome have planned or attempted suicide in their lives and as many as 66 per cent have entertained thoughts of suicide.

Depression can reveal itself in many forms and the triggers vary from one person to another. Here, I will make the point that while we can easily recognise symptoms of depression, sustained as they are over time, we can also be lured into thinking that its similarities with autistic traits will allow similar strategies to be used – or one to be diagnosed over the other. Both conditions may, for instance, be associated with rigid thought patterns, disturbed sleep, changing eating habits, solitary behaviour, communication difficulties, sensitivity to environmental stimuli, non-functional routines, poor self-awareness, limited interests and limited emotional affect. However, I think it would be very unwise to treat a person with the co-morbid conditions of autism and depression as if she only had depression. Imagine trying to 'cheer up' a depressed autistic teenager whose autism means she struggles to read and understand body language even when she's not depressed. Imagine trying to encourage another teenager to talk about her feelings when she is unable to recognise and interpret these at the best of times. Depression and autism are complex partners and therefore require special consideration when devising programmes of support and intervention.

How we can help

If you suspect your child is suffering with depression, then you will need to seek appropriate professional support in the first instance, perhaps through the family GP or local Child and Adolescent Mental Health Service (CAMHS). The following ideas are not prescriptive and are for reference only.

1. Throughout this book, you will find references to autism-friendly environments. For children who are vulnerable to episodes of depression, these environments will also need to be mood friendly, that is, mindful of the conditions that trigger episodes and the conditions that can pre-empt them. This might involve adults being resilient role models, synchronising demands to levels of tolerance or creating sensory spaces (that children enjoy according to their interests).

2. A team around the individual should be beneficial in the sense of identifying the adults who can support the child and support each other. These adults will have a clear understanding of the nature of the young person's depression – how this manifests in or is entwined in her autism. They should also have an agreed way of anticipating difficulties, be able to monitor changes in her mood or behaviour, and be consistent in their responses to concerns.

3. Where counselling or therapy is considered, make sure that the professional is experienced in supporting children with autism. Without this experience, I think it is harder for professionals to see the situation through her eyes and to fully appreciate the depth of her worries and anxieties (e.g., if they seem minor in conventional terms). It will also be harder for professionals to communicate in a way that is meaningful to the individual or to propose truly realistic goals (i.e., goals that accommodate the inflexible and perseverative nature of autistic thinking).

Where we can go next

* Attwood, T. and Garnett, M. (2016) *Exploring Depression, and Beating the Blues*. London and Philadelphia, PA: Jessica Kingsley Publishers

The book, like the title, is divided into two parts – with an initial exploration of depression (why it can occur and how it presents in people with Asperger syndrome) and then a ten-part intervention programme, which can be completed privately at home or with a trusting adult.

* Dubin, N. (2014) *The Autism Spectrum and Depression*. London and Philadelphia, PA: Jessica Kingsley Publishers

Nick is an adult with Asperger syndrome who has periodically suffered with depression. This book explores the reality of depression in the context of the autism spectrum and considers different ways of managing it.

17. The Power of Hating
(A poem about low self-esteem)

> *Thoughts*
> *Negative, charged*
> *Circulating, expanding, separating*
> *The power of hating*
> *Myself.*

What we can learn

When I was a Master's student in 2008, I studied a module that focused on curriculum innovation and I remember a tutorial comparing syllabuses from different countries. It was interesting to see how individual subjects were influenced by matters such as culture, religion, history and governance, and also to explore the ways in which subjects were taught. Ten years on, I would be curious to know what changes there have been and whether these reflect, in the UK at least, the increasing need to promote children's wellbeing.

Wellbeing encompasses many domains and is all too frequently discussed in the context of children with autism – children who are referred to services because they have low self-esteem, self-harm, talk about hurting themselves or have tried to kill themselves. These issues are not prompted by autism (i.e., are not experienced by every person with autism and can occur in people without a diagnosis) but there are certain aspects of the autistic profile that make some individuals more vulnerable than others. Children who are rigid thinkers, for instance, will not easily be persuaded that their negative personal assessments are incorrect. Those who seek absolute perfection will find it hard to regard the inevitable setbacks of life as anything other than devastating failures – *or* may avoid telling people that there are problems just to save face. Children who act without anticipating consequences can inadvertently drive away or incite their peers (e.g., feeling isolated or being bullied without knowing why) *or* they can unknowingly put themselves at extreme risk (e.g., refusing to eat or trying to cut themselves). In other ways, children with autism are vulnerable if they do not recognise their emotional state or relate this to their current behaviour. They may not realise that what they are thinking, feeling and doing is unhealthy, they might not know how or when to stop and they might not realise that someone can help them. If they do know that a person can help, they might not have the communication skills to communicate what the problem is. This poem paints a picture of such a person – someone who has internalised herself as a failure and who cannot escape or communicate the harmful thoughts that perpetuate this belief.

How we can help

1. Providing support for children who regard themselves in a persistently negative way is not easy and can be distressing. Whatever strategies you use with your child, be committed and act positively – persevering even when you feel little progress is being made. Thought habits are hard to break and children typically show resistance when changes (new strategies) are introduced. You can only make headway if you project an aura of belief in what you are doing and have the fortitude to see it through.

2. It may seem trite to recommend a balanced diet, regular exercise and restful sleep but in my experience, they really do go a long way to alleviating the symptoms of low mood. Important building blocks in fitness and in health, these factors encourage greater positivity by helping children feel *physically* better. When they feel good physically, they are physically stronger to deal with problems.

3. Try setting small goals for your child that help her experience success and gain a sense of achievement, no matter how small. Make sure the goal spans a realistic timeframe and celebrate successes in a visual way where appropriate, for example with a certificate, sticker or token (but think ahead and be prepared to deal with the moment when a goal is not met).

Where we can go next

* Karim, K., Ali, A. and O'Reilly, M. (2014) *A Practical Guide to Mental Health Problems in Children with Autistic Spectrum Disorders*. London and Philadelphia, PA: Jessica Kingsley Publishers

  An informative guide explaining different types of mental health problems that can present alongside a diagnosis of autism. Each co-morbid condition is defined and illustrated, and important points are highlighted. Various treatments and strategies are recommended at the end of the respective chapters.

* Musgrave, F. (2017) *The Asperger Teen's Toolkit*. London and Philadelphia, PA: Jessica Kingsley Publishers

  Part 2 focuses on wellbeing and includes topics relating to depression, anger, substance abuse and self-harm.

Chapter 9

CONVERSATION SKILLS

18. Train of Thought
(A poem about reciprocity)

*Let's go on a journey and call it a conversation
We'll both take the tube and start at one station.
Your carriage will head straight on the black London line
While mine branches left, confused by the signs.
I'll try to keep up and shadow your track
But watch for derailment as I take up the slack.
Carriages will fill with words, comments and questions
Leading to rush hour and unwanted congestion.
Service may reduce and perhaps be suspended
Causing lengthy delays till my circuits are mended.
Yet once the conductor has signalled all clear
We'll set off once more, in a slow forward gear.*

What we can learn

A few weeks ago, I was browsing in a bookshop and stumbled across a title on the London Underground. It was full of quirky facts, and my favourite was the one that identified the only tube station containing none of the letters in the word mackerel: St John's Wood. It's something you can check for yourself the next time you're in London waiting for your tube or you're in transit pressed up against a carriage door. And while you are looking at the map, allow yourself a certain train of thought – that the network of lines could be a visual metaphor for how an autistic person processes a conversation. In my interpretation, the start and end of any line would be the start and end of a particular conversation, with each station representing points and parts of it. The distance between stations would reflect the time taken for the person to process an idea and to relay or interpret it. We can then imagine that if the train (i.e., conversation) is begun by the child, it is likely to follow a designated linear route, where particular words and phrases are used in a familiar way. We can also imagine, however, that if the conversation is started by the other person, that the train's departure is essentially unannounced and she has to work out which station it started from (creating a delay or conversation pause). As the conversation ensues, the child and the other person will be on the same train, but if they are a distance apart, problems will arise when it's time to switch trains (i.e., change topic) or when the child leaves in search of a more comfortable train (e.g., goes off on a tangent or stops talking due to demand overload).

Reciprocity in conversations is notoriously problematic for children with an Asperger syndrome profile, since they can be easily distracted, not realise that they are meant to say something in return, want to talk exclusively about their own interests, not pick up on body language or struggle with timings (e.g., may interrupt, talk at length or need longer to respond). They can also interpret literally (missing jokes, idioms and sarcasm), use a monotonous tone, echo things they have heard, and speak with repetitions or scripting (e.g., randomly repeating chunks of words heard somewhere else). When I'm having a conversation with someone, I seem to quickly derail with thought tangents

– for what the person says often makes me think of something, which makes me think of something else, and makes me think of something else again. So, like the person in the poem, I'm having a thought conversation with myself while trying simultaneously to have a spoken conversation with the other person.

How we can help

1. Trains are often appealing to children on the spectrum and have lots of scope to explain elements of conversation in metaphorical terms. Joel Shaul's book *The Conversation Train* (2014) provides us with a rich example of this. If trains are of no interest to your child, then the principle at least may be helpful – using an individual's special interest to identify teaching points. Computer-based explanations, for instance, might use the idea of opening one program at a time to explain turn-taking, or the idea of avatars to explain speaking styles, or the idea of levels to explain how and when to change topics.

2. Conversation truly is an art, which needs to be practised. Freestyling spontaneity is important, but makes it harder to develop particular skills. Remember that children are often preoccupied with parts rather than wholes so it makes sense to dedicate time to teaching specific elements (greetings, turn-taking, tone, phrases, personal space etc.) which can be practised and put together in different conversation scenarios. If we (sensitively) draw attention to the aspects they need help with, then they at least know what to work on.

3. Be mindful of distractions in the environment. Background noise, the number of people in the vicinity and the type of location you are in (shop, classroom, corridor, kitchen) are

just some of the factors potentially affecting the person's ability to concentrate on what you are saying and to engage in a reciprocal manner.

Where we can go next

* Newman, J. (2017) *To Siri with Love*. London: Quercus Editions Ltd

Judith is a parent of twin boys, one of whom is on the spectrum. Her book is full of wry, amusing and heartfelt anecdotes that demonstrate many of the conversation traits identified with Asperger syndrome – including literal interpretations, thought tangents, repetitiveness and a preoccupation with special interests.

* Shaul, J. (2014) *The Conversation Train*. London and Philadelphia, PA: Jessica Kingsley Publishers. (Original work published in 2010 by Autism Teaching Strategies.)

A clever book using trains as a visual metaphor for teaching different aspects of conversation to children on the spectrum. It is divided into two sections, with the first focusing on the elements involved in a conversation and the second providing a range of worksheets. Part Three in Section One is called 'Staying on Track'.

19. Heated Conversations
(A poem about talking in groups)

Entering a space full of people
Inflamed with conversation
Is like opening a hot oven
So acute is the sensation.

Words blast in my face
And make me spin on my feet
To avoid getting burned
I have to retreat.

Silence begets comfort
And is worn like a cape
Extinguishing the fire
Once I've made my escape.

What we can learn

Have you ever been late for an appointment, a meeting or a course and tried to slip in or catch up quietly without being noticed? Can you remember the last time you arrived at a social function with apologies for your delay (e.g., to a party, wedding or meal)? Do you get embarrassed when a group of people suddenly turn to look at you? Autistic or not, most of us should be able to relate to the potential awkwardness of these scenarios, either through past experience or a recent occurrence. What our poem shows us, however, is that the reaction and response from a person with autism can be more intense than average – a reaction probably familiar to many of you already.

Assembly halls, classrooms, dining rooms and playgrounds, indoor play centres, supermarkets, waiting rooms and front rooms – these are but a few of the spaces where people congregate and children can panic. Their verbal responses and physical reactions will indicate that the moment is stressful but they might not explain why. It's hard to explain a problem if you struggle to communicate *and* you are feeling anxious. For some children, it will simply be the noise or rather the mass of noise (hearing separate sounds all at once), while for others it will be the sudden feeling of claustrophobia (even one person can be overwhelming). Some will feel the pressure of having to say something (regardless of whether a person has addressed them) and automatically freeze, temporarily losing their voice and coherent thought. Some children will be thrown by the idea that everyone is looking at them and pace to and fro in their mind about whether to bolt or hide. When I enter a small and busy space, it is the layers of noise that affect me most. The combination of competing sounds and the multiplicity of conversations invade the silence in my head and leave it gasping for air. My fingers clamp shut, my skin prickles and my body tenses with a wave of frustration and the force of social expectation. Encountering a group where several conversations are afoot really is like springing back from the heat of an open oven.

How we can help

1. Children sometimes cope better with loud noises in social spaces if they are given opportunity to occupy the space first and for the noise to grow as people populate it (rather than facing the noise of an instant crowd).

2. Try to introduce some form of structure that makes it easier for the child to manage. This could include a transition activity – something that overrides the pressure to join in immediately and that she can do while acclimatising – such as organising a resource in class, setting up her workspace or

sitting quietly with a preferred object. It could also include reference to a script or a 'group conversation' protocol, specifically telling her what to do.

3. Be sensitive to the child's difficulties but also generous with your 'can do' approach. This is not only about the language you use (positive, encouraging and reassuring) but also about preparation – that the individual knows what to expect, that this suits her current mood, and that she has access to the item or activity that helps her feel secure (such as a learned phrase, headphones or fidget object).

Where we can go next

* Coelho, A. (2017) *Sometimes Noise is Big*. London and Philadelphia, PA: Jessica Kingsley Publishers

A picture book written for children aged 5 and over, it shows the reader how someone with autism can experience the sensory environment. A companion guide is also available for parents and professionals.

* Cotugno, A.J. (2009) *Group Interventions for Children with Autism Spectrum Disorders*. London and Philadelphia, PA: Jessica Kingsley Publishers

This book may be of particular interest to staff in schools wanting to set up a social skills group for older children as it provides relevant theoretical and practical information, and includes some templates for creating pupil profiles.

20. Just Saying
(A poem about blunt speech)

Why is she so fat and wobbly?
Why's his nose so big and blotchy?

Why's her hair all painted blue?
Why's his arm got that tattoo?

Why is she so old and wrinkly?
Why's her breath like coffee, stinky?

Why can't that girl stand up to walk?
Why can't that boy use words to talk?

Why d'you always redden and wink –
When I'm just saying what I think?

What we can learn

One of the more equivocal traits associated with autism is a predisposition towards plain speaking, directness and honesty – characteristics that may be admired, amusing or troublesome depending on the situation. Children with autism often say precisely what they think without realising that their opinions may be ill-timed or challenging to others, or that these lack subtleties of application (e.g., a child who is told off for telling people they smell, then uses the phrase 'My mum says I'm not allowed to say you smell'). It's as if children have a thought filter that operates on a different programme, literally saying what's on their mind regardless of who they are talking to, how this might be interpreted or how it could affect a friendship. It is not generally a spiteful habit, which would imply the individual understands it will embarrass or upset the person (different from remarks that provoke a known reaction), but it can be something that children find hard to keep in check for a number of reasons. How can you organise what you say if you are unaware that the meaning of words may be multiple and changed by tone and context (e.g., 'You look nice' can be complimentary or sarcastic; stern voices can be disapproving or assertive)? How can you relay empathy if your understanding of emotions is somewhat limited (e.g., describing someone as fat without anticipating their upset or embarrassment)? Why would you alter what you want to say if you neither understand social hierarchies (e.g., that we conventionally address adults and peers in different ways) nor audit your thoughts for social approval? Good communication skills are inherently social, and social success generally stems from the interplay of the two. If we know that 'social' is challenging for children on the spectrum, we can see further why a child might make comments like those in the poem.

How we can help

1. While a conversation about 'a conversation' has the potential to be a challenging exercise, it can be facilitated by stories, pictures, cartoons, illustrations, written words and role play – visual tools that help the individual see (rather than imagine) how her comments make people feel. The visuals should vary according to the child's age, cognitive ability and previous experience. Be careful not to underestimate her literal interpretation of the material, however, and know that her understanding will need to be supported by practice in situ. Children are good at learning rules but may only apply them to the original stimulus (i.e., they know what the 'answers' are to the pictures but struggle to remember or apply them in a real situation).

2. Comic strip conversations are the invention of Carol Gray and help children understand a person's behaviour by means of guided questions and simple drawings. They allow children to describe a moment as they saw it and to see what other people were thinking and feeling – learning how the situation could play out in another way next time. So, if a child speaks plainly in a way that is hurtful to someone, she can see how this made the person feel and learn how to manage this in future.

3. If you know that a child routinely finds it hard to filter what she says despite your best efforts, try teaching her different ways of greeting people and how to pay a compliment. She may have a genuine interest in speaking to the person but not know any other way to start a conversation other than to describe what she observes.

Where we can go next

* Gray, C. (1994) *Comic Strip Conversations*. Arlington, TX: Future Horizons

   Carol's short and concise guide explains what a comic strip conversation is, how it is formulated and how it is used. There are photocopiable versions of the different tools involved and you can find picture examples on the internet.

* www.blacksheeppress.co.uk

   Black Sheep Press produces a pack called *Talking About Conversations*, which can be purchased from its website. The pack is designed for secondary school-aged children and consists of pictures, scripts and strategies focusing on different scenarios. The pack can be used to help children develop social interactions and communication skills.

Chapter 10

LITERAL THINKING STYLES

21. Exhausted Over Time
(A poem about the abstract nature of time)

Time does not fly, it's not a bird
It can't be lost or pressed
And I don't see how it is spent
Or stood to take a test.

Time can't run out, it's not a pen
It can't be kept or guessed
But one thing that I know is true
I now need time to rest.

What we can learn

During my last group holiday, it amused me to hear fellow travellers quizzing the tour leader about the days ahead, needing to know in advance what we were doing and when (and crucially, the time that we would leave in the morning). Away from home, they were suddenly dependent on a stranger to give their day structure and, tacitly, a sense of security – dealing with new places and unfamiliar people, and practices they were unacquainted with. It was amusing because of its striking resemblance to that of a person with autism travelling (metaphorically) through daily life, wanting certainty and order in an uncertain and disordered world. People with autism deal with time in different ways and the functionality of their strategies or responses depends on their level of understanding and how this has arisen. Some children are perpetually anxious about the immediate or distant future and will repeatedly seek reassurance, asking the same questions about an event until it is upon them. Others are reputedly present-orientated and only preoccupied with the here and now. In the poem that inspires this piece, we can see that our child regards time as a mystery and is bewildered by its meaning in different contexts and by its intangibility.

How we can help

1. Processing time or thinking time, whatever you call it, is a valuable commodity and its merits cannot be overstated. None of us copes very well with overload but we may anticipate its arrival and take steps to manage it. Try to remember that a child with autism will not be able to do this in every given moment and reaches her processing threshold more quickly than you can see or she expects. Make sure that you avoid bombarding or overwhelming the person with too much language or information and give her the gift of time to think and respond without you interrupting (or repeating yourself). Count to 10 in your head if it helps!

2. If your child fixates on time and repeatedly asks questions about when something is going to happen, set limits as to the number of times the question can be asked. I have found this works better than verbal tennis, answering the question ad infinitum (since this reinforces the behaviour and increases anxiety). You can set the limit in the course of the exchange

and rely on the person to mentally keep track, or you can mark these visually, for example with tokens (if your child is a serial questioner, you could make this a general strategy – always carrying a set of say five tokens, which are exchanged for each question asked in a given moment).

3. Time is an abstract concept but can be made more tangible and visible through devices like clocks, watches, stopwatches, traffic light cards (stop, get ready, go), numerical scales, finger countdowns, instruments (associating routines with sounds), schedules, calendars and of course timers (egg, sand, bubble or electronic). Sand timers are very popular but think about how and when you use them. If necessary, have timers in sight but not in children's hands, and try using direction arrows and end marks for those who like to turn the timers prematurely.

Where we can go next

* Higashida, N. (2017) *Fall Down 7 Times. Get Up 8.* London: Sceptre. (Original work published in 2015.)

Naoki is a young adult with autism and this is his second book. Part 2 is entitled 'Time and Life' and provides some personal insights in this area.

* Rogers, L. (2013) *Visual Supports for Visual Thinkers.* London and Philadelphia, PA: Jessica Kingsley Publishers

Chapter 3 is about schedules and gives some practical advice on how to get the most out of them. While focused on classrooms, the examples are easily transferable to the home environment.

22. Don't Make Me Wait

(A poem about waiting)

I want it NOW, not in a tick
Don't make me wait
Or I'll be sick.

I need you NOW, not in a sec
Don't make me wait
I'll hit the deck.

I must leave NOW, not in a mo
Don't make me wait
Or I will blow.

What we can learn

Waiting is definitely not a joyful experience for many of the children I support at home or in school. Whether they are waiting for the start of an event, the adult's attention, to end an activity, or to be given something they want, waiting can be an intense source of upset, confusion, worry and frustration. Remember the last time you were placed on hold during a phone call or put in a caller queue, and then exaggerate your impatience by one hundred. You might now be in the region of emotion felt by children who have little understanding of time or indeed an appreciation of why they have to wait in the first place. If you or the toy is there, why can't you help or give it to me? Waiting is a difficult skill for young children to learn, particularly because of the language conventions used, their tendency to look inwards (rather than appreciate other people's needs) and because of their difficulty controlling impulses (unable to hold back). Children can learn to wait but only with our support and understanding –

which may be a big ask when the child's request is at odds with the situation, when an argument or tantrum erupts, or when you are in full view of public eyes. Just as children need to learn patience, so do we in terms of knowing that the child's skills will improve over time.

How we can help

1. Try giving your child something to focus on while she is waiting – and where possible, offer the distraction before you know the wait will occur. Dealing with the problem in advance should mean helping the child when she is more receptive. So if you know that she routinely demands your attention when you are cleaning or cooking the tea, provide the distraction before you begin. If you know that she always wants to be the first to leave the carpet area, then act before carpet time ends. The distraction should be motivating and tangible rather than verbal. I know a colleague who sometimes recommends using a 'doorstop buddy' with young children, as these are heavy to hold (a tick for sensory regulation) and are commonly made in the shape of an animal (which may be appealing and could have a name).

2. Start with a realistic goal for teaching your child to wait, and decide how long this moment might last and when you will practise it. When the moment is staged (e.g., you are deliberately pausing before giving your attention), support this with a visual prompt – such as a timer, wait symbol or amber card – and then provide the attention as soon as the waiting time is over. If you do this often enough, the child should learn to trust that she will have what she wants when the visual is used. Once this link has been made, you can start to increase the waiting time and practise waiting in a wider range of situations.

3. Be mindful of your body language and how you speak to her when she has been told to wait. If you appear frustrated, this will project onto her and amplify her own existing frustration. If you use time-related words, make sure she understands what these mean and be true to your word. If *you* don't do what you say, why should she?

Where we can go next

* Devine, A. (2016) *Flying Starts for Unique Children*. London and Philadelphia, PA: Jessica Kingsley Publishers

Chapter 12 provides lots of useful information on how to teach waiting skills to young children and includes case studies, strategies and top tips.

* www.pinterest.com

A good place to be inspired by other people's ideas, there are a wide range of weighted options to be found when using 'weighted objects and autism' in the search bar.

Chapter 11

INSISTENCE ON SAMENESS

23. Black and White
(A poem about black and white thinking)

Stop go
Then fast and slow
Ups and downs, smiles and frowns
My head's full of contradictions
Yes no?

What we can learn

I really must brush up on my TV soaps and pop stars. My niece, nephew and I played Twenty Questions at the weekend and challenged each other to guess the name of a celebrity with only yes/no answers as our guide. The 30-plus age gap between us didn't help, nor the fact that I still didn't know the person when they told me. For the record, I was a gracious loser. I start with this anecdote because it highlights a wonderful tension between the rigidity of 'black and white' approaches and the challenge of choice. Wouldn't it be easier if we were told what to ask? (The boundaries in this instance would be helpful.) But then, aren't the simple limits of a yes/no answer remarkably *unhelpful*? Wouldn't you want the person to show some degree of flexibility – to offer some type of clue? Black and white approaches are a known characteristic of thinking styles on the autism spectrum and clearly have their advantages and disadvantages. In some respects, it's an admirable quality to be so sure of your judgement and determined in a certain course of action. Besides, how many people do you know who don't have a strong view on something, be that politics, exercise, animals, marriage or raising children? Mind you, I would imagine that they are not always immune to different possibilities and are more flexible at other times, say in less important or familiar contexts. When it comes to autism, black and white thinking means thinking literally and being *routinely* unaware of different shades of possibility and adopting this as a 'go to' approach. From the child who insists on particular routes, wants food served in only one way and demands the same toy or seat, to the child who refuses to do school work at home, views herself in a negative way or believes that she is always right, these patterns of behaviour are, in essence, the black and white yes and no outcomes of situations that are otherwise as bewildering as Twenty Questions. Black and whites are comforting because they provide a more certain outcome in any given situation. The more predictable this is and the more control the child has over it, the better; it's 'safer' to stick to the same behaviour. To consider other possibilities is to risk confusion, overload and a dent to self-esteem. We shouldn't say that children are unable to process different possibilities but we should consider the motivation for their singular responses and be creative in our own.

How we can help

1. For children who insist on sitting in the same place all the time (e.g., on the sofa at home, a corner of the dining room,

on a certain table), try linking the place to a more portable object such as a cushion or a placemat. In this way, she can learn that her place is always where the object is rather than a static location.

2. Solution-focused discussions may work with older or more verbal children as these encourage them to consider more than one possibility. As an example, if you have a teenager who only eats upstairs, you can explore this as a positive and negative (e.g., I can still play on my computer versus I will have smelly food in my room) and then work through other options (e.g., I could eat with my family at breakfast or I could eat my dessert downstairs) which equally identify their pros and cons. When this technique works, the adult will have skilfully led the child to the more desirable behaviour but made it seem that she has chosen it (rather than being told).

3. Black and white thinking can sometimes show itself in more subtle ways, such as by speaking in opposites or 'deliberately' doing the wrong thing to provoke a reaction from adults. Children who read the wrong word in a text, incorrectly label objects or colours, write the wrong answer or contradict what you (and they) know is true are all possible scenarios. If your child insists on speaking in opposites or deliberately gives the wrong answer, try calling her bluff and following suit, for example if you are reading a story and say the wrong word on purpose, she may feel impelled to correct you.

Where we can go next

*   Shaul, J. (2012) *Flexibility in Kids with ASD – Card Activity to Teach this Social Skill to Children on the Autism Spectrum.* Autism Teaching Strategies. Accessed on 15/01/18 at www.autism teachingstrategies.com/autism-strategies/flexibility-in-kids-

with-asd-card-activity-to-teach-this-social-skill-to-children-on-the-autism-spectrum

There are lots of autism-friendly resources on Joel's website and this particular resource, downloadable for free, addresses the area of flexible thinking.

* Shaul, J. (2016) *Our Brains are Like Computers!* London and Philadelphia, PA: Jessica Kingsley Publishers

A visual guide helping children understand people's thoughts and feelings. Part 6 includes a variety of games and templates, which can show individuals what other people thought or how they felt after something that happened.

24. A (Not Very Fine) Rainy Day
(A poem about repetitive behaviour)

Press down. Push up.
Push door. Door shut.
Press down. Push up.
Push door. Headbutt.

Off, on. Off, on.
Light off. Light on.
Off, on. Off, on.
Light off. Bulb gone.

Tap off, tap on.
One drip, then flow.
Tap off, tap on.
Stop rain. Please go.

What we can learn

How many of you agree that there's no such thing as bad weather, only bad clothing? And does this reflect your own feelings towards the outdoors or your child's? Fair weather or foul, like it or not, we all know that there are times when we can't do what we want – and that there are times when going outside is just not an option: it's toilet time, there's a lesson starting, the tea is on, or you're getting ready for bed. Many children love being outside and feel frustrated when they are not. Part of this frustration arises because they don't understand why they are allowed out in one instance but not in another. Increasing frustration can lead to an angry outburst or reveal itself in intensely repetitive behaviours. These are organising for some but an indicator of anxiety in others; in both cases, they serve as a coping mechanism. Repetitiveness plays a key role in the diagnosis of autism and can include the tendency to switch things on and off, turn taps, pull on levers, flush toilets, lift up or drop parts of clothing, line up objects, repeat words, sounds, phrases or questions, perform certain movements (like hand flapping or bouncing) or insist on the same routes when travelling. Some of these behaviours can become part of elaborate rituals that children have to complete before the next event or activity and are fearful of breaking. This need for control and order is something that children can desire without realising it. In this example, we have a child who is desperate to go outside but can't because of the weather. Told to stay inside, she acts on the belief that if she keeps trying the door, it will eventually be opened. When this fails, she moves on to a pattern of behaviour that reflects her efforts to fill the time and keep calm.

How we can help

I. Fix a double-sided picture prompt on the door at the child's height. One side will show the rain and the child indoors (either as a cartoon or an actual photograph of her), the other will show dry weather and the child outdoors. If pictures are confusing, you could simply use red and green colours in the manner of stop and go, displaying the side that is relevant in the moment. Make sure you refer to the green side whenever she goes out so that this visual prompt is used all the time (not just when the weather is poor).

2. Set up a rainy-day box that contains special items likely to appeal to your child and that are only used on wet days. For pre-verbal children, the box would serve as an object of reference for a particular routine, helping them know what to expect and what to do when they can't go out. The box may include a favourite DVD, CD, book, magazine, toy, game, jigsaw, wordsearch and so on.

3. Try using red crosses to deter children from touching switches and door handles (or climbing up on things), placing them in relevant places around the room. These can be surprisingly effective with some children as they explain in a clear and visual way that some places or things are not accessible.

Where we can go next

* Higashida, N. (2013) *The Reason I Jump*. New York, NY: Random House

Originally published in Japan when Naoki was 13, this book provides a fascinating mix of short narratives written as answers to questions 'typically' asked of someone on the spectrum; there are a number of questions and answers relating to repetitive behaviours. A screen version of this book is apparently in the making.

* Moor, J. (2008) *Playing, Laughing and Learning with Children on the Autism Spectrum*. London and Philadelphia, PA: Jessica Kingsley Publishers

Julia has lots of ideas for play and for supporting play, and these include wet play and activities indoors.

Chapter 12

ATTENTION
TO DETAIL

25. The Magic of Three
(A poem about focusing on patterns and details)

The monkeys wise. Hard to look in your eyes.
Billy Goats Gruff. Being social is tough.
Neapolitan ice cream. Emotions not what they seem.
SOS code. Sensory overload.
Traffic (circles of) light. Pressure means flight.
School legged race. Need a safe space.
Red, white and blue. Each moment like new.
X Y Z in a vector. Read rules like the Ofsted Inspector.
Bronze, silver and gold. Hard to do as I'm told.
Goldilocks' bears. Prone to danger and dares.
Wheels on a trike. Specific like.
Robin reliant. Might look defiant.
PDA. Mean what you say.
Christmas French hens. I like knowing the 'whens'.
Rock paper scissors. Thoughts run like fast rivers.
Group of blind mice. Visuals are nice.
Maggie, Lisa and Bart. Reward chart.
The Condition ASC. The magic of three.

What we can learn

I remember seeing an episode of *The Autistic Gardener*[1] where Alan Gardner (the designer) finds inspiration for part of someone's garden hidden in the quadrilateral created by the passing blades of two adjacent wind turbines. People on the spectrum are renowned for their capacity to focus on details and can spot patterns that others regard as inconsequential or indiscernible (until they are pointed out). These details and patterns are not necessarily graphic and can be rooted in light, movement and sound. Think about the children who like to watch the light shining through their fingers as they wave them in front of their face. Or the children who are transfixed by the movement of falling leaves, rising bubbles or flushing water; the children who compulsively tap or spin objects, or use the same phrases and vocalisations over and over. Though they might be trying to regulate a sensory need, they might also be fundamentally exploring patterns in the world. Daniel Tammet's (2013) book *Thinking in Numbers* provides us with a rich and academic example of how to appreciate numerical patterns and details, explaining how numbers play a crucial (and perhaps unconscious) role in many areas of daily life.

How we can help

1. Where appropriate, celebrate children's observations and use them as a means of promoting functional interactions, communications and applications. If a child is fascinated with logos, you could help to collect samples in an album and draw their attention to labels on food or care labels on clothes. If a child likes to watch the movement of objects, you could

---

1   *The Autistic Gardener* (2017) [TV] Series 2, Episode 1. UK: Channel 4

compile a treasure box of related objects while introducing toys with moving parts. If a child concentrates on the light through her hands, join in alongside and experiment with other colours or sources of light through tubes, prisms and material.

2. An ability to notice details can have great advantages but also poses a challenge if the focus of attention is in conflict with the task at hand. In this instance, you may need to acknowledge the behaviour or thought that has been presented first, but explain what the child should be attending to now. Visual explanations will be more useful on the whole, such as a timetable showing the child that she should concentrate on X first and then Y.

3. Remember and promote the phrase 'different not less'. More socially aware children or teenagers, for example, may feel that they need to hide their thoughts and observations to avoid drawing attention to themselves, or have their creative potential inadvertently stifled by conventions aimed at standardisation.

Where we can go next

* Tammet, D. (2013) *Thinking in Numbers*. London: Hodder and Stoughton. (Original work published in 2012.)

A book containing short but readable essays on the presence of maths in everyday life.

* Tammet, D. (2017) *Every Word is a Bird We Teach to Sing. Encounters with the Mysteries and Meanings of Language*. London: Hodder and Stoughton

Daniel has a gift for languages as well as numbers. The first chapter is called 'Finding My Voice' and indicates how his passion for writing was ill-fed by his experiences of high school education.

Chapter 13

SPECIAL INTERESTS

26. Reading the Landscape
(A poem about reading)

Lift the cover and escape through the door
Leave Lonely behind, don't let him follow.
Now I can breathe. The air smells sweet and pure
And the view is so lush, my eyes wallow.
In the distance I sense gates beckoning.
Fingers become footsteps that twist and turn.
Familiar paths ease the reckoning.
Must keep on forward, to strive and discern.
Absorbed in landscapes, irritations cease.
Freedom is comp'ny, roaming how I please.
Words often contained find gentle release,
Whispering with a literary breeze.
My Sun runs to greets me, at last I'm home.
Solitude smiles mirroring my own.

What we can learn

Reading is a common pastime for children but can be particularly enjoyable for those on the spectrum. Books truly offer an escape from the demands of social life and not least because they are reassuringly structured, repeatedly available and tailor-made to a person's interests. Women and girls on the spectrum are typically fans of reading and their reading serves different purposes, for example as a manual for learning how to 'fit in' (memorising phrases, studying fashions or modelling people's characteristics), to become experts on a special interest or simply to relax. Children can spend many hours absorbed by a book and become so engrossed that the outside world fades away – seeing, hearing and feeling the words and pictures on the page, but not the sights, sounds and emotions of people in the environment. While reading might be described as something solitary, paradoxically, it could equally be interpreted as something companionable. Do you think a child feels alone when she is reading? I don't think so. But she might do if she was in a crowd of people. Perhaps for many individuals with autism, reading is the time when they feel least alone. Hence the poem. Here we have a child who opens a book and finds herself transported to another place – a paper landscape if you will. Just as we sense new smells in new countries (e.g., when disembarking a plane), so the smell of the pages is exotic and reviving to her. The pages become part of her travels and she uses her fingers to walk along the sentences. Reading helps her feel calm and relaxed, and stops her thinking about social judgements, criticisms or faux pas. The feeling of peace allows her to think, say and do without fear of reprisal; she can be herself and enjoy being by herself. To her, this freedom is company enough.

How we can help

1. Whether you are at home or in school, you can turn reading into a social experience by sharing in your child's interest and her love of reading, for example quietly reading your own book alongside her, reading the same books as she is,

commenting on her book (at the right moment) or discussing it with her.

2. Showing an interest in your child's reading habits is important – ensuring that what she is reading is age and content appropriate (especially with teenagers and the internet), and that her understanding of what she is reading is morally and emotionally sound (i.e., is not likely to prompt risky behaviour or cause anxiety).

3. Early readers and young children on the spectrum can develop interests in books that are couched in set routines and repetitive behaviours, for example lining up books, continuously flicking through pages, taking the adult's finger to point to pictures, waiting for the adult to use specific phrases, endlessly wanting to read the same book or focusing on particular parts. When you are introducing books to children, try to develop a routine that you are comfortable with and one that can evolve; it's easier to change your routine than the child's. Visuals such as timers, Social Stories™, choice cards, turn cards, finished boxes and reading rules can be useful.

Where we can go next

* Hoopmann, K. (2000) *Blue Bottle Mystery*. London and Philadelphia, PA: Jessica Kingsley Publishers

There are lots of books available today that feature characters on the spectrum. Children with autism may enjoy reading about those they can perhaps intuitively identify with. Kathy Hoopmann, for example, has written a number of story books about children with Asperger syndrome and this is one of her earliest. It centres on a boy called Ben, his friend Andy and their ensuing adventures following the discovery of a bottle in the school playground. The story is written in such a way as to reveal some of the traits that come with the diagnosis.

* Suskind, R. (2014) *Life, Animated. A Story of Sidekicks, Heroes and Autism.* Glendale, CA: Kingswell

In this book, covering a 20-year period of family life, Ron Suskind shows us how his son's interest in Disney films became a vehicle for learning and for expressing and managing his emotions. It's a fascinating example of how important and problematic special interests can be for a person with autism.

27. Billy the King
(A poem about music and singing)

I'm Billy James and love to sing
Elvis[1] is my favourite thing.
'In the Ghetto' ten times a day
'All Shook Up' in every way.
'Caught in a Trap' just like the king
'A Little Less Conversation' this does bring.

What we can learn

I am never going to be a musician even though my infant teacher told me I have the hands of a pianist. The only keys my fingers will ever dance over are those of my computer. Even if I had the inclination, I would be scuppered by my inability to read

---

1   Words encased by speechmarks in the poem refer to the titles and/or lyrics of Elvis songs, which feature on the (2013) album *The Nation's Favourite Elvis Songs*

music. A music score is as baffling to me as an encryption code, so I have the utmost admiration for people with any musical ability. An aptitude for or special interest in music is in fact fairly common on the spectrum and even exists as a therapy, nurturing musical talent and important skills in communication and social interaction. For some, the association with music is all encompassing[2] and embedded in a successful career. In modern times, Susan Boyle and James Durban are two exceptional examples, while historically, Mozart himself may have been autistic. For most individuals, however, the gift of music is idiosyncratic but no less sustaining. These are the children who spontaneously sing the lyrics to songs but find it hard to talk. Children who can accurately hum the tune of something they have heard only once but won't imitate peers. Children who can draw musical instruments with amazing clarity but struggle with daily living skills, and further, those who develop fascinations with music genres, bands and artists much sooner than you would expect – a nod to the youngsters who love rock, opera or Motown, The Beatles, Abba or Elvis. Indeed, music can become an obsession in some instances – an absolute need to sing, dance or play the same album, track or song over and over. Sometimes six rounds of a pop song or nursery rhyme simply might not be enough. Where language has developed, children may only want to talk about their favourite music or only respond when this is proffered. In some cases, children may be so absorbed by their own interests that they reject other suggestions no matter what the form – frustrated with the car radio, parents singing or songs in assembly, for example. 'Billy James', therefore, is our model for the children who adore a certain type of music, who

---

2   If you are familiar with the television drama *The A Word*, you will have seen how the character Joe uses music to drown out the social world and/or to keep calm (see *The A Word* (2016) [TV] UK: BBC1)

repeatedly succumb to its charm and who, significantly, achieve a level of mastery that others might not have deemed possible.

How we can help

1. For early learners, try encouraging sounds and words with microphones, recording devices and karaoke videos. A microphone provides opportunities for turn-taking (copying and extending each other's sounds), while recordings invite interest and joint attention. Children's music videos often have the added benefit of teaching movement and signing – developing coordination, communication and knowledge of parts of the body.

2. Rather than seeing the behaviour as something restrictive, one option would be to channel the child's interest in songs and music so that this is not only enjoyable to her but also a basis for acquiring new skills. You could expose her to a range of instruments or begin with something like an electronic keyboard, which is easy to use and accompanied by pre-recorded melodies.

3. Try using her love of music to extend her listening and attention skills, for example with sound books, sound games, audio books, dance mats and interactive computer consoles.

Where we can go next

* Berger, D.S. (2016) *Kids, Music 'n' Autism*. London and Philadelphia, PA: Jessica Kingsley Publishers

Dorita has spent more than two decades teaching music to children on the spectrum. Her book has nine chapters divided into three parts, which collectively emphasise the importance of music to children and the different ways in which children of all abilities can access music.

✻ Elder Robison, J. (2016) *Switched On*. London: Oneworld Publications

In 2008, in America, John (an adult with Asperger syndrome) was introduced to a brain therapy called transcranial magnetic stimulation, which explores the reading of emotions in others. One of the experiences he describes in the book refers to his sudden ability to feel emotionally connected to music. You can read about this in the chapter called 'The Night the Music Came Alive'.

28. LEGO® Set
(A poem about LEGO®)

I've
Built a
Tower with
The LEGO® bricks.
I used six blues and four reds and ten clicks.
I emptied the box to find the best picks
And left a mess
That you'll
Need to
Fix.

What we can learn

LEGO® seems to be one of those timeless toys that finds its place in the company of both adults and children and it is reckoned that there are an average of 80 bricks for every person on the planet (National Geographic Kids 2017). So it's hardly surprising that LEGO® is also found in the company of individuals with autism – and consequently regarded with devoted fascination due to its uniformity and precision, its relationship with TV and film and its capacity to draw the player in with the utmost of concentration.

LEGO® has been explored as a therapy for children with autism for more than a decade now and, as an intervention, was first described by Daniel B. LeGoff in 2004. His research showed that LEGO® could be used to develop a child's interaction and communication skills by working collaboratively with others in structured tasks, where children assumed different roles, took turns and communicated information as a small group. I've used LEGO® therapy in the past with some of my own pupils and was impressed by the effect it had on them – they were so focused on the activity that they learned valuable social skills without even realising it. LEGO® is certainly an attractive medium for youngsters and therefore one prone to highlight strengths and potential problems. I have known children who are able to build complicated models without referring to a guide, seen children who play LEGO® videos on repeat, watched children restrict their attention to particular bricks and arrangements, observed children panic at the thought of their prized model being touched or dismantled, and worked with children who tip everything on the floor to find the few pieces they want.

How we can help

1. Use small boxes with lids and limit the number of bricks to a manageable amount. More bricks to play with means more bricks to tidy up.

2. Provide picture cards with (new) ideas of things that children can copy and make, or create templates for designs that children can match onto directly.

3. Set up an area for storing models and label these with 'best before' dates so that there are planned and finite intervals for when the child's creation will be displayed before being put away.

Where we can go next

* LeGoff, D.B., Gómez de la Cuesta, G., Krauss, G.W. and Baron-Cohen, S. (2014) *LEGO®-Based Therapy*. London and Philadelphia, PA: Jessica Kingsley Publishers

   Daniel's initial book presents the theory behind the approach and explains how a programme of LEGO® intervention can be designed and implemented.

* LeGoff, D.B. (2017) *How LEGO®-Based Therapy for Autism Works*. London and Philadelphia, PA: Jessica Kingsley Publishers

   A follow-up to the original work, this book uses a series of case studies to show how effective the therapy can be for children with autism.

PART 2

IN SCHOOL

If someone mentions the word school to you, what does it make you think of and are your thoughts positive or negative? I imagine it will depend on your present circumstances. If you work in a school, then your responses will perhaps centre on the challenges of your job, the colleagues you work with and the children you support – presumably influenced by how well things are going and how far into the term you are. If you are a parent of a child with autism, however, then your responses will probably depend on whether or not your child is enjoying school at the moment.

In 2006, The National Autistic Society published a report that was part of a campaign to *Make School Make Sense*. It was based on the views of more than 1200 parents and 25 children and ultimately highlighted key differences in the experiences of families who were either satisfied or dissatisfied with the understanding and support their children had received in education. Contributing factors were identified as barriers in the types of provision that children could access, the amount of training staff received and the approaches that schools used. These barriers were naturally challenged with a raft of recommendations, with the authors stating that:

Access to an appropriate education can maximise the life chances of individuals with autism... All children with autism have the potential to learn, achieve and make a positive contribution to school life...good practice...enables them to do so. (Batten *et al.* 2006, p.44)

In my work, I regularly have opportunity to ask children what they think about life in their primary or secondary school and, while their responses often reflect the idiosyncrasies of autism (e.g., based on the latest special interest or a historical problem not yet resolved in their minds), they also indicate the relative fragility of their 'school' happiness. That this can easily be affected – in either direction – by the relationships they have with their peers, the current perceptions they have of themselves and the support they receive from adults.

I see many children who enjoy school and do well. These are children who, as I see it, are accepted and included in their school community, where efforts ensure that problems are spotted and dealt with early on, where support is in place to enhance engagement, and where parents and staff work together with a real understanding of and sensitivity to the child's strengths, interests and needs. This understanding and sensitivity means that, in more cases than not, adults are better placed to help children celebrate the good and tackle the difficult. Maybe, just maybe, the following poems will help you, the reader, gain a little more insight into what this might entail.

Chapter 14

TRANSITION

29. The School Run
(A poem about starting school in the morning)

When you say goodbye, I'm filled with terror
It makes me feel you're leaving forever.

If I can't see you, you're no longer here
I feel all alone and tremble with fear.

How will I get home and when is later?
It's all so confusing – What d'you mean 'alligator'?

Why say goodbye if it makes my tears flow?
And if I hold on so tight, why d'you struggle, then go?

What we can learn

Many children can find the separation from parents stressful and struggle to understand why they are being 'left behind'. Children with autism are no exception but may take longer to adapt because of their thinking style and learning habits. Reasons for the distress will vary from one child to another but probably all have something in common – namely a difficulty with thinking flexibly and seeing the bigger picture. Children may not appreciate why they 'suddenly' have to come to school and cannot stay at home; they may not have had enough time to deal with the morning routine (or to finish something they like); they may be anxious about the children and staff who are part of an environment they have little control over; and they may not have a meaningful grasp of time and thus an understanding that the adult will return eventually. Children with autism don't automatically consider new ways of reacting to a situation they find hard, as if their way is the only way of leading to a more desirable outcome.

How we can help

1. Parents and staff should work to establish a clear and consistent morning routine so that the child can predict when she is going to school and knows what will happen when she arrives and the parent leaves. (This may or may not involve arriving earlier or later than the usual start time to avoid the busiest part of the day.)

2. The child may benefit from access to a quiet area and/or opportunity to start with a favourite activity in the immediate minutes after the adult has left. Consistency in this regard may be of particular merit to children who do not always arrive at the same time each day; adults can give them a particular task or activity to do so that their day always starts the 'same' regardless of the time they arrive.

3. In most cases, it is important for the adult to say goodbye, rather than leaving quietly without the child noticing. Adults should behave in a positive and non-alerting way – indirectly showing the child that there is no cause for worry.

Where we can go next

* Autism Education Trust (2016) *Autism Standards*. London: Autism Education Trust. Accessed on 31/07/17 at www. aettraininghubs.org.uk

  Available as a pdf download, this document sets out the standards that reflect good practice in four main areas: The Individual Pupil, Building Relationships, Curriculum and Learning, and Enabling Environments. It is compatible with the Special Educational Needs and Disability Code of Practice and the Common Inspection Framework.

* Bradley, R., Jones, G., Milton, D. and Kerem, M. (2014) *Working Together with Your Child's School. An AET Guide for Parents and Carers*. London: Autism Education Trust. Accessed on 25/02/18 at www.aettraininghubs.org.uk/wp-content/uploads/2014/07/AET_working_together_with_childs_school.pdf

  Also available as a download, this guide enables parents and carers to prioritise what is important for their child through a series of ratable statements. Each section concludes with links to further reading and suggested resources.

Chapter 15

EARLY PLAY SKILLS

30. Thomas
(A poem about a fascination with trains)

Forward and back, forward and back.
Pushing my Thomas
Along the train track.

Forward and back, forward and back.
My wonderful Thomas
Goes clickety clack.

Forward and back, forward and back.
Move away from my Thomas
Or I'll go on attack.

What we can learn

In the 20 years that I've been working in the field of autism, I have probably seen as many toys and interests as I have encountered children with the diagnosis. Technology has undoubtedly had a massive impact on the way that children (of all ages) now like to occupy themselves – whether that's using the latest smartphone or tablet, claiming the interactive whiteboard as their own or animating a new Disney figure. But one thing that has endured without the wifi or flat battery is the omnipresent fascination with magnetic trains or Thomas the Tank Engine. I'm sure there are many reasons why this is so, but from an autism perspective, perhaps it's because trains have a comforting element of repetition, for example in the number of wheels (numerous and doubled), the way that they move (forward and back) or the track that they run on (commonly on straight lines or curves). If trains lend themselves to repetition, then it's little wonder that children who use them tend to engage in repetitive behaviours – running the same sequence over and over without getting bored. Their fascination and preoccupation with trains and repetition, however, can create problems when others want to join in. I have observed many children who are possessive about their trains and who vehemently reject advances from others – assuming their train will be taken or their play ruined.

How we can help

1. Help the child broaden the scope of their interest in Thomas the Tank Engine by introducing them to relevant stories, magazines, CDs, colouring books and so on. It may take some time for the child to shift her attention to these resources but adult efforts should be rewarded through quiet persistence, for example regularly leaving an item close by for the child to see or modelling how to use it.

2. Try playing alongside with your own set of trains, copying what she is doing and then, by demonstration, suggest different things that could be done, such as building a tunnel and pushing the train through it, sitting figures on the train and pushing it, or stopping the train at a station and fixing it. Over time, you can begin to offer her pieces to see if she will join in with your play or change her own.

3. Display Thomas-style rule cards in the area of play, stating, for example, how many children can 'visit the station' (play), which trains 'can be driven' (shared) and when the train journey 'ends' (tidied up).

Where we can go next

* Al-Ghani, K.I. (2011) *Learning About Friendship*. London and Philadelphia, PA: Jessica Kingsley Publishers

This is a book containing a number of stories that can be used to teach specific concepts. Story 5 is about a boy who is fascinated by Thomas the Tank Engine.

* Plummer, D.M. (2008) *Social Skills Games for Children*. London and Philadelphia, PA: Jessica Kingsley Publishers

Deborah's book provides both theory and advice on teaching social skills to children and describes a multitude of games that can be explored in groups.

31. Pop-Up Toy
(A poem about playing with adults)

They call it a face
I know it's a toy
It has a button and trapdoor
That bring me all sorts of joy.

The nose makes a noise
When I give it a press
Each time I do it
There's a new sound to guess.

Sometimes I touch it and
A trapdoor is sprung
It pops out of its mouth
This thing they call tongue.

Then the mouth closes tight
With my finger inside
But as soon as I wiggle
The door pops open wide.

Yet the thing I like most when
I play with this toy
Is when the voice goes all funny
And says 'Who's a clever lil boy?'

What we can learn

I once saw an illustration that compared children's play in modern times with play in times past. The first cartoon showed a muddy child reluctantly being pulled indoors, while the second showed a child on a tablet being reluctantly pulled outside. Certainly, with the technology and the jazziness of toys at our disposal today, it is easy to overlook the simple pleasures of fun and games, and assume that play means having lots of equipment and expensive items. This can be a particular temptation for parents or staff – buying multiple versions of a toy or numerous sets as soon as they spot their child's interest. Many of you will know, however, that when it comes to play, the toy that catches and holds children's attention is not necessarily a toy in its truest sense, nor assuredly used in the way you would expect. Our poem gives us one such example – where a child is fascinated by parts of the adult's face but treats these as distinct objects rather than parts of a person. At first glance, the child's play and the interaction between the two may look fairly typical and conventional. It's not unusual, for instance, for babies and infants to press and pull and poke – but they do this to build the interaction with a *person*, not to make the *objects* repeat their action. Children who treat parts of the face as individual 'toys' may focus on these without the accompaniment of eye contact, which would enable them to gauge the adult's reaction or to smile in anticipation. Moreover, children may also act in this way with anybody, indiscriminately sitting on a stranger's lap to touch their face.

How we can help

1. Children's songs are often rich in actions for movement and can be used to teach the names of different parts of the body and face (and thus how to reference these in a functional way). Be mindful of the pace of the songs that you choose, however, as children will need processing time to coordinate what they hear with the movement required. Children may need to hear a song a number of times and be supported by an adult modelling the actions.

2. There are lots of toys that children can use to develop their understanding of parts of the face and body, such as teddies, dolls, small world figures, Mr Potato Head, jigsaw puzzles, Play-Doh people, Thomas the Tank Engine or Fuzzy-Felt. You could use these as an appropriate distraction if needed. When using the toys, try to make reference to the body in a functional way, for example when playing with a doll, you could point out that baby has closed her eyes and gone to sleep.

3. If your child persistently wants to touch your face, you could try sitting beside her in front of a mirror – allowing her to touch parts of your reflection instead. You could invite her to find the same feature on her reflection (That's Sarah's nose. Where's your nose?), introduce face paints to accentuate the parts, or wear novelty props (wigs, hats, giant sunglasses, red noses etc.), assuming these are not aversive.

Where we can go next

* Stock Kranowitz, C. (2003) *The Out-of-Sync Child has Fun. Activities for Kids with Sensory Integration Dysfunction.* New York, NY: The Berkley Publishing Group

While this book focuses on sensory processing difficulties, it is still a useful source of inspiration for activities implicitly promoting interactions and developing an understanding of different parts of the body.

* www.ginadavies.co.uk

Gina Davies is a practitioner in the field of autism and this website provides information about an approach called Attention Autism, which is divided into four phases developing skills in attention and social interaction.

32. The Trouble with Sharing
(A poem about skills and sharing)

I will not share because
This is not my chair
Under me.

I will not share because
You changed your hair
I see.

I will not share because
I feel your stare
Burn me.

I will not share because
I do not share
For free.

And how can I share
If you're not prepared
Consistently with me?

What we can learn

This is another example of how children with autism can focus on a particular detail when learning a new skill and how this affects their ability to apply the skill in different situations. In the figurative sense, we could represent a skill as the final image of a jigsaw, which can only be completed when all the pieces fit together and none are missing. So, as a child acquires a new skill (like sharing) this may be based on the assemblage of certain details that must be present when the skill is required next time round. The instructing adult may not realise that the child's difficulties completing the puzzle (implementing the skill) are due to the fact that some of the pieces (attributes) she focused on at the time of learning are now missing in the current context. In this poem, I have imagined a child whose efforts to share are hampered by changes in the environment that she interpreted as essential when sharing – for example, her seat is not the same and the adult's hairstyle is different.

How we can help

1. Aim for some measure of consistency when teaching a child to share so that the activity becomes familiar and predictable, for example using specific resources, working in a designated area or saying particular phrases. As the child makes progress, so these variables can be altered to generalise the skill.

2. Practise with multiple and physically distinct items in the first instance and allow children to select their own portion, such as choosing an animal from a tub, a biscuit from a box, a crayon from a pot, a song prop from a bag. The child may cope better when the sharing activity is practised on a one-to-one basis and then extended to include other children.

3. The sharing of one item may be more successful when the focus item has a neutral status. It sounds obvious, but I often see strategies on play plans relating to the use of favourite items. While this serves as a means of attracting the child's interest, it also has the potential to elevate stress levels in an already stressful situation (i.e., interacting with others and parting with something deemed precious).

Where we can go next

* Gray, C. (2010) *The New Social Story*™ *Book*. Arlington, TX: Future Horizons

  A Social Story™ is a versatile tool, developed by Carol Gray and widely used with children on the spectrum to explain a social situation and their engagement with it. There are many examples in the book and story 62 is about sharing.

* Moor, J. (2008) *Playing, Laughing and Learning with Children on the Autism Spectrum*. London and Philadelphia, PA: Jessica Kingsley Publishers

  Chapter 2 covers issues relating to attention and sharing.

33. All Mine
(A poem about possessiveness over toys)

You
Think I'm
Difficult
But I am not.
These toys are all mine and you just forgot.

What we can learn

This poem gives us an example of how children with autism can differ from their peers when it comes to understanding possessions. It's not uncommon for children – any children – to have an attachment to a particular object that they are unwilling to part with or share, but most will generally have some understanding that their behaviour is unfair when other children are referred to. They may not like the adult's intervention, but will probably learn from it. When a young child with autism views her environment, she views it through *her* eyes rather than the people around her – not automatically able to consider the impact of her actions on others. Instead, she will be more focused on making sense of and exploring the objects that are attractive to her, inadvertently developing unhelpful habits. She may like objects to stay in the position where she first remembers them and become intensely anxious when these are moved by someone else, as if this 'displaces' her sense of order and calm. Try imagining how you feel when someone uses your favourite mug or seat in the staff room, when your keys aren't where they should be or when you forget where the car is in the car park. Now inflate those feelings infinitely and begin to imagine how the child with autism experiences objects in her environment – how panic ensues when things are 'taken' by others, or not where she thinks they should be.

How we can help

1. Set up a small box or tub containing a nominal selection of the toys that the child generally favours and decorate it with her photograph/name/favourite images. This will make it easier for adults to explain which toys 'belong' to her and which ones are for other children (or siblings).

2. Use a timer or traffic light cards to show children how long they can play with a particular toy – helping the child who is attached to the object *and* the child who is waiting for or having her turn with it. Turns may be necessarily short to begin with but then increase in length as children become more tolerant.

3. Try introducing a Toy Menu that states the main Toys of the Day and rotate these on a regular basis so that children have less opportunity to develop fixations with particular items.

Where we can go next

* Howlin, P., Baron-Cohen, S. and Hadwin, J. (2003) *Teaching Children with Autism to Mind-Read*. Chichester: John Wiley and Sons Ltd. (Original work published in 1999.)

Through a series of black and white illustrations, this book invites children to think about the emotions that are inferred in different contexts.

* Schectman, T. (2012) *20 Visual Timers for Children with Special Needs*. Michigan: Friendship Circle of Michigan. Accessed on 02/02/18 at www.friendship circle.org/blog/2012/11/06/20-visual-timers-for-children-with-special-needs

This link should lead you to an inventory of timers, showing the range of types available and where to source them.

Chapter 16

FASCINATIONS AND SPECIAL INTERESTS

34. Sticky Fingers
(A poem about Blu Tack)

This blob of blue is just the best
The best that's been invented.
I like to stretch it in my hand,
It makes me feel contented.
You hide it under pictures
And in a metal pot.
You hide it in your big desk drawer
Where my hands are found a lot.
I like to play your hiding game
To seek my sticky tack,
But I love it most on Monday morn,
When I open up your brand-new pack.

What we can learn

The sticky putty that we know of as Blu Tack has long been a fascination for autistic children who like to collect it, taste it, mould it, bury things under it or busy their hands with it. It's one of many items that children like to hold in their hand and may be regarded by some as a comforter, satisfying a sensory need. Objects in the hand can, however, also serve as a welcome focus point for children who struggle with unstructured time (it gives them something to occupy themselves with) or, conversely, with structured time that is led by an adult (when they are expected to do something they don't want to do). This concentrated fascination may have an additional benefit in that objects largely seem consistent in how they look and feel, and seem more predictable than people. Perhaps this sense of sameness helps to alleviate anxiety in what children otherwise consider confusing or overwhelming contexts.

How we can help

1. Children who are fascinated with Blu Tack can be provided with a small container that shows how much is available for use and where it can be obtained. They can be directed back to this source whenever they try to take Blu Tack from places deemed out of bounds (e.g., wall displays).

2. For younger children, it may be appropriate to mark areas with 'no entry' cards, showing where Blu Tack must not be removed, while for older children, it may be more appropriate to introduce a specific rule or replacement activity.

3. Try using a work station for children who struggle with unstructured time in lessons. A work station is essentially a place free of visual distractions, where the work to be done is clearly identified and completed in a highly structured way. Given a new focus point, children may feel less need to seek Blu Tack.

Where we can go next

* Mesibov, G. and Howley, M. (2003) *Accessing the Curriculum for Pupils with Autistic Spectrum Disorders*. London: David Fulton Publishers

   Chapter 6 explains and illustrates how work systems are set up and used in more detail.

* Verdick, E. and Reeve, E. (2012) *The Survival Guide for Kids with Autism Spectrum Disorders*. Minneapolis, MN: Free Spirit Publishing

   Part 3 has several chapters focusing on ways of managing feelings and relaxing.

35. Pink
(A poem about a fascination with colours)

Ribbons, spoons and multilink
How I love the colour pink.
Eyes wide open, must not blink
I stare and stare to help me think.

What we can learn

A child's fascination with objects can be demonstrated in a variety of ways. Apart from a need to hold them in her hand, you will probably also notice certain patterns as to the colours and numbers of objects she chooses, for example always wanting to hold 'three' objects or homing in on the colour pink. Typically, you will also notice the unique ways in which she likes to study her objects, such as staring intently (or squinting) at what she regards as the most interesting detail. Moreover, when she focuses on the objects she may position herself very closely, holding them up to her face, squat down to study them on the table at eye level or lie beside them on the floor. If she is very stimulated or excited by the objects and her actions (e.g., pushing or spinning them), she may also flap her hands, jump up and down or repeatedly move backwards and forwards.

How we can help

1. Consider whether the objects are helping or hindering learning in order to determine the most appropriate response – avoid making automatic assumptions about whether the child should have them or not. Responses may focus on reducing the quantity and frequency, or on enhancing and replacing.

2. To encourage variety or flexibility, gradually increase exposure to other objects by building on emerging themes, for example if the objects of interest are easily spun, then spinning may be the schema to begin with. In the first instance, the introduction of new objects may simply involve them being available, helping the child get used to them being there (before being encouraged to use them).

3. Try using colour as a 'special interest' in activities to provide an alternative means of helping the individual develop the skills being targeted, for example sorting, building, nesting or posting 'pink' versus other coloured objects; using 'pink' writing tools in mark-making; drinking and eating with 'pink' utensils; or using visual aids backed in pink paper to support communications.

Where we can go next

* Beckerleg, T. (2009) *Fun with Messy Play*. London and Philadelphia, PA: Jessica Kingsley Publishers

  If you are looking to broaden your child's play interests, you could consider ways of introducing messy play. Here Tracey explains why messy play is important and suggests resources that can be used.

* Todd, S. and Gilbert, I. (eds) (2015) *The Little Book of the Autism Spectrum*. Carmarthen, Wales: Independent Thinking Press

  Chapters 7 and 15, respectively, discuss autism-friendly environments and repetitive behaviour.

36. (Season 22) Phonics
(A poem about the spectrum of special interests)

Sound buttons 'dr-ew'

Robot arms and Dr Who

Cybermen 'fl-ew'

Mutating Daleks 'gr-ew'

Lost in Season 22.

What we can learn

In this poem, we have a child who has her own way of joining in with a phonics lesson, drifting into thoughts of her special interest. While her peers are pretending to be robots whose arms slide up and down with the sounds of a given word, she is thinking about Dr Who. Special interests, as we have seen, are typical in the presentation of autism and can be as varied as the spectrum is broad – sharks, trains, the Victorians, natural disasters, books from the Ladybird series, radios, flags, TV gardeners and Harry Potter to name but a few. What sets them apart from general interest in a topic is the manner in which they are researched, shared with others and applied to everyday life. Children will often invest long periods of time finding out as much as they can about a topic that interests them and display an intensity of concentration that contrasts starkly with their span of attention elsewhere. The 'research' process is generally concerned with gathering detailed facts that can be committed to memory and recalled verbatim when required. Children, in essence, become mini experts in their chosen subject – knowledgeable in areas that might be considered strange to their peers or improbable given their age. While this expertise is advantageous in certain domains (e.g., is personally calming, used as an incentive to complete a task or imparts knowledge to those without the knowledge), it can also be disadvantageous (e.g., monopolising a conversation or taking over a task that has been set). Children may, for instance, talk in monologues and *at* a person, not knowing that their speech doesn't make sense to the listener (through incoherence or the person's lack of knowledge), they may 'forget' that the listener has heard the information many times before, or they may be unable to interpret their knowledge in the face of questions.

How we can help

1. With careful management, special interests can be harnessed in functional and useful ways, for instance they can become the theme of tasks that children might otherwise find mundane (e.g., creating 'superhero' maths sheet or basing a Big Write on dinosaurs). Or they can be used as an incentive to do the task itself (e.g., 'Once you have finished your spellings, you can colour in your shark picture').

2. The concept of a special interest could be developed throughout the class so that everyone has opportunity to investigate and share their own at varying points across the timetable. This implicitly celebrates differences and different interests (typical or otherwise) and can be implemented in a variety of ways, such as allocating five minute slots on a rota basis or displaying written work on an identified noticeboard.

3. If you are teaching a child to blend and segment words, you could demonstrate this visually as well as orally by using letter cubes that connect together, jigsaws with a letter per piece, or letter beads that can be threaded on a string.

Where we can go next

* Attwood, T. (2015) *The Complete Guide to Asperger's Syndrome.* London and Philadelphia, PA: Jessica Kingsley Publishers. (Original work published in 2007.)

   Chapter 7 provides lots of information about special interests, including their breadth and functions.

* Jackson, L. (2004) *Freaks, Geeks and Asperger Syndrome.* London and Philadelphia, PA: Jessica Kingsley Publishers. (Original work published in 2002.)

Luke has a diagnosis of Asperger syndrome and in this book, talks about life as an adolescent. Chapter 4 concerns 'Fascinations and Fixations', while Chapter 9 illustrates his experiences at school – with reference to reading.

37. Baa Baa Angry Birds
(A poem about computer games)

'Baa baa time to stop
Let's play another game.'
'No miss. No miss
Want to play the same.
Once for the pictures
And once for the words
And once for the sound effects
That go with Angry Birds.'

What we can learn

Many children with autism are highly motivated by tablets and demonstrate high levels of concentration when using an app of their choice. A tablet is one of many tools that can help children learn useful skills, but should be encouraged with caution as it doesn't always lend itself to positive interactions with others and can become an object of fixation. Moreover, the way that children engage with the apps is not always purposeful, for example showing repeated patterns of tapping and scrolling, opening and closing, or replaying favourite parts over and over. The desire for repetition is captured in this poem, and shows how some children, once engrossed, find it hard to finish and move on to something else.

How we can help

1. Model how to use a new app by playing alongside the child on another tablet. This will help her see the features within the program and how they are used without interfering with her own. Over time, you should see a growth in her interest, curiosity and trust, such that she watches what you are doing, reaches out to join in with you, or even takes it over as her own.

2. Set limits as to how long she can use the tablet – whether this is for her own enjoyment or as part of a teaching activity. The longer she is left to entertain herself, the harder it is for her to finish. Help her recognise when the time is drawing to an end in a visual way – using repeated warnings if necessary.

3. Use picture cards on a timeline to show her when she can use the apps she desires and/or use a choice board to show what options are available. Ensure that there is a substitute task ready when the end comes so there is a new focus or means of distraction.

Where we can go next

* Hardy, C., Ogden, J., Newman, J. and Cooper, S. (2002) *Autism and ICT*. London: David Fulton Publishers

  This is a guide for teachers and parents, which discusses ICT in the early years and suggests practical strategies.

* Kutscher, M.L. (2017) *Digital Kids*. London and Philadelphia, PA: Jessica Kingsley Publishers

  A comprehensive guide to the use of technology today, comprising sobering statistics, explanations and strategies. Chapter 7 includes information about screen time in the early years.

Chapter 17

CLASSROOM DEMANDS

38. Look and Listen
(A poem about dual processing)

'Look into my eyes'
She says, so I can listen.
She's not very wise.

She should say 'ears',
Because when she looks at me
SHE never hears.

What we can learn

Eye contact is something we are 'programmed' to do from an early age and soon becomes a social convention to maintain interactions with others. When we look at another person, we are indirectly telling them that we are listening and are interested in what they are saying, and expect that they will reciprocate. If eye contact is 'missing', then we assume the opposite. How many times have you found yourself saying, 'Look at me when I'm speaking to you', for instance? Eye contact is one of the non-verbal behaviours specifically highlighted in autism, and difficulties can include: inconsistent eye gaze, avoidance, indirect gaze (e.g., looking at the person's mouth or glancing sideways on), staring too intently and a lack of joint attention (i.e., not looking at something that is pointed out, nor initiating this). Children may or may not be aware of these difficulties, either because they are so absorbed in their own activity and can't shift their attention, or because they are anxious. Children's awareness may also be complicated by issues relating to multi-sensory processing. This poem, for example, concerns a child who cannot deal with auditory and visual information at the same time, becoming confused or overwhelmed when trying to do 'two' things at once (to look *and* to listen). Some children find it easier to concentrate on what they can hear when they don't have to look at the speaker directly.

How we can help

1. Be mindful of children who find it hard to process and integrate visual and auditory information when you are giving instructions. A child may respond better if you show her the task first and then explain what to do instead of doing the two things at the same time.

2. When teaching social skills directly, try providing the person with a generic point that she can focus on during interactions, such as her partner's eyebrows or forehead, or over the person's shoulder.

3. Some children may find it easier to concentrate or listen in class if their seating position is in a particular place, for example at the back to maximise physical distance, or to one side to make use of their peripheral vision.

Where we can go next

* Elder Robison, J. (2009) *Look Me in the Eye. My Life with Asperger's*. London: Ebury Press. (Original work published in 2007.)

  A personal account of John's journey through childhood at a time when the condition was 'unknown'.

* Verdick, E. and Reeve, E. (2012) *The Survival Guide for Kids with Autism Spectrum Disorders*. Minneapolis, MN: Free Spirit Publishing

  Chapter 10 helps to explain some of the basic skills involved in communication, including eye contact.

39. Too Much Information *Squared*

(A poem about demand overload)

'Quickly sit down.'
'Get your things out.'
'Answer your name.'
'Please do not shout.'
'Come to the carpet.'
'Bring your whiteboard and pen.'
'Repeat after me.'
'Now tell me again.'

'Work with a partner.'
'Move over there.'
'Count with the cubes.'
'Raise your hand in the air.'

'Tidy away.'
'Just listen and wait.'
'Go back to your table.'
'Use the short date.'

'Don't write in the margin.'
'Miss out the next line.'
'Show me your working.'
'You are doing just fine.'

'Check all your answers.'
'Keep your hands to yourself.'
'Copy this down.'
'Leave the things on the shelf.'

'Make that your last one.'
'Oh no... Come sit next to me...'
'Let's play a new game...'
'Just breathe nice and deep-ly.'

What we can learn

This is a poem about a child with PDA struggling to cope during a maths lesson, but could equally be about any child on the spectrum since those with an autism or Asperger syndrome profile can also have difficulty coping with demands and discharging stress. In this present scenario, the demands of a lesson are hidden in the instructions and phrases used by the teacher, which accumulate as invisible stresses until panic results. The poem reminds us that children who are quiet are not necessarily coping – that their anxieties could be just as extreme as those associated with socially manipulative and disruptive behaviours. Staff teaching children with or without PDA, therefore, must be hugely intuitive in their approaches and must know the child well enough to reduce the likelihood of overload and to facilitate engagement by assessing and determining how many demands are manageable in any given moment. This poem provides 28 examples of statements that could easily be construed as 'too much information' – a strapline that The National Autistic Society used in one of its campaigns in 2016 (The National Autistic Society 2016), drawing public awareness to *sensory* processing difficulties. The campaign showed how sensory information in the environment, which may be indiscernible to many, can impact on people with the condition, essentially prompting flight, fright or fight responses to escape demands on their sensory systems. Where the poem is entitled 'Too Much Information *Squared*', I am envisaging a child whose ASC diagnosis already equips her with a vulnerability to environmental and situational demands, but that these are magnified by her PDA profile.

How we can help

1. Ensure that there are adults who know the child well and understand that her ability to cope with demands will vary from one day or one moment to the next. A 'team' around the child should promote positive relations by virtue of staff taking turns to support the person and the individual having opportunity to start afresh on a regular basis.

2. Work with the child to create a safe space that she can retreat to when needed – but present the discussion as a suggestion so that the ideas seem to be offered as her own (rather than obviously directed by the adult).

3. Think about the phrases that you use in conversation with the individual and try to state these as invitations that essentially make her look good. Imperatives such as 'should' or 'must' are likely to be unhelpful and lead her to think she is not the person in control. Potentially, demands could be disguised

as phrases like 'Would you like to…?' 'I wonder if you could help me…?' 'Can the blue table do…?'

Where we can go next

* Fidler, R. (2016) 'Exploring PDA.' Nasen magazine. *Special.* November edition, 26–27

In this brief but informative article, Ruth summarises the key characteristics of the condition and identifies some helpful strategies.

* Sherwin, J.A. (2015) *Pathological Demand Avoidance Syndrome. My Daughter is Not Naughty.* London and Philadelphia, PA: Jessica Kingsley Publishers

A highly readable book charting a mother's account of her daughter's difficulties during her early and primary years. Part 2 focuses on school.

40. The Graceful Swan
(A poem about accumulating stress)

You could be forgiven for thinking
I'm a graceful white swan
But look under water
There's a lot going on.

If fish are demands
I'll eat them all day
Moving swiftly to catch them
Swimming each and all ways.

I may look ever hungry
But it's just a disguise
Too many of your fish
Tip me over. Capsized.

What we can learn

One of the icebreakers I like to use in my training sessions is a counting game that instructs adults to alternately count to three in pairs. Over three successive rounds, I replace the numbers with actions so that people are eventually clapping, stamping and gesturing instead of counting. It produces plenty of laughter and then thoughtful discussion when I invite suggestions as to the skills that this game requires. Some are obvious, like remembering instructions and taking turns, while others are less apparent, like being flexible or judging personal space. The point that I always make, however, is that any activity involves an unexpected degree of implicit demands, which are not necessarily appreciated or taught until one of them surfaces as a problem. Children with autism may struggle with the finer details of tasks before they've even attempted the task itself: you could think of this as effectively doubling, tripling or quadrupling their workload. The teacher may set the class some work to do at the table, for instance (like writing a newspaper article), but not realise that this 'one' task is veiled by need to: organise the resources required; share desk space with a group of other children; tune out the noise of the projector; reference source material and process it; produce a physical response; and cope with interruptions. And none of these demands may have been listed at the outset.

How we can help

1. Timetable regular breaks during the day and at strategic points in a session to temper stress levels and reduce pressure points (even if it doesn't look like she needs them). Breaks do not have to be lengthy or resource heavy but should involve movement, for example delivering a message, giving out equipment, reading a favourite book, sharpening pencils, or using an object that she can manipulate in her hands.

2. Aim for some measure of familiarity when introducing new topics or teaching skills so that the 'newness' is contained within a smaller remit and gives the person one less thing to think about, for example working in a particular place, using a specific writing tool or starting with a mini whiteboard.

3. When a child is overloaded, remember that her thinking and communication skills will be operating at a lower level than usual. Rather than asking questions about what is wrong or telling her what to do, *model* what needs to be done, for example, 'Let's take five deep breaths', or 'Let's go to your den'.

Where we can go next

* Aspden, K.L. (2016) *Help! I've Got an Alarm Bell Going Off in My Head!* London and Philadelphia, PA: Jessica Kingsley Publishers

  This book has been written for children who find it hard to manage their anxieties, and is presented in four short and illustrated chapters.

* Van Gelder, E. (2015) *I'm Not Strange, I have Autism.* The Netherlands: Village/VanDorp Publishers

This book provides an adult's interpretation of her life on the spectrum and the challenges she faces. Her 26 topics are listed under letters of the alphabet. The section on feeling 'Exhausted' is short but illuminating in the context of this poem.

41. All That Glitters
(A poem about Golden Time)

Monday morning, feeling nervous
Almost five whole days to go.
Will I get my Golden Time?
Shame I do not know.

Tuesday break time, feeling scared
Three whole days to go.
Lost my favourite Stickle Brick
And had a fight with Joe.

Wednesday lunchtime, feeling worried
Two full days to go.
Too noisy in the dining room
Lost my temper so.

Thursday late and disappointed
One big day to go.
Missed out on a smiley face
My work pace was too slow.

Friday pm, so excited
No more days to go.
Why's it hard to earn my time?
Shame I do not know.

What we can learn

Golden Time features in many primary school classrooms and is often timetabled at the end of a week, celebrating the work that has been achieved and signalling a final break from lessons. Children have the opportunity to play with resources and choose their own activities. It's a time that can be immensely enjoyable and hugely worrying for a child with autism. Some schools, for example, use the time as a motivation for good conduct, assuming that the promise of minutes and time with a favourite item will deter children from behaviour others consider inappropriate. Children may be given opportunities to earn points, dojos, tokens and so on that are exchanged for free time, but have these removed when their behaviour is poor. Unfortunately, a system such as this assumes that a child is able to regulate and manage her behaviour, and will predict and understand the consequences of not doing so. A child with autism is not always able to do this, reacting to situations instinctively as and when they occur. Golden Time can create great anxiety in her mind if she knows that she is expected to 'behave' every day but finds it hard to control her emotions. Seeing points/time lost for incidents as they happen, while other children appear only to be earning them is in itself a potential trigger. The poem shows how Golden Time can almost have the opposite effect to that which it intends – where points of stress build up and time awarded falls.

How we can help

1. Develop a custom of praise and rewards that is embedded in day-to-day practice, not just highlighted as a weekly occurrence. Children should learn that Golden Time is a special part of the timetable and not the sum of it, that effort and behaviour can be acknowledged in many and varied ways.

2. Set personal, achievable and visible goals for the young person so that she knows *how* to earn points, tokens or minutes for Golden Time; goals may be represented as rules on her chart or as symbols in her work space. Stating the ways in which she will accrue time explicitly gives her more control about when the items are awarded and focuses on positive rather than negative behaviour.

3. Plan for the children who find Golden Time stressful, for example by using a timer or a timetable, organising a quiet space to concentrate or using rules to state the behaviour expected.

Where we can go next

* The National Autistic Society (2015) *Autism. A Resource Pack for School Staff.* London: The National Autistic Society. Accessed on 14/07/18 at www.autism.org.uk/professionals/teachers/classroom.aspx

This pdf document covers a range of classroom topics and can be downloaded from the webpage listed – by scrolling down to the bottom of the page.

* Clements, J. and Zarkowska, E. (2004) *Behavioural Concerns and Autistic Spectrum Disorders.* London and Philadelphia, PA: Jessica Kingsley Publishers. (Original work published in 2000.)

Chapter 10 discusses components of motivation and how these can be affected or effected.

Chapter 18

LITERACY SKILLS

42. The Importance of Pictures
(A poem about using pictures and symbols)

Picture cards are really great,
They let me have a voice.
You put them on the table top
So I can make a choice.

Pictures help me know what's next
And later through the day.
I like to know when work is done
And when it's time for play.

You can put them in my picture book
Or mount them on the door.
You can put them on a special board,
But don't keep them in your drawer.

What we can learn

I once visited a local museum and read an information panel that was entitled 'Pictures are Powerful'. The writer justified this by saying that pictures enable access to complex situations and help people think, learn and understand. I would agree; they are an invaluable means of interpreting and making sense of the world, whether for personal reference or on a social level. And they are certainly a brilliant way of supporting individuals who struggle to communicate with others, developing their ability to 'talk' in the absence of words or full sentences. In communication systems, pictures are typically represented as symbols, photographs or drawings and used to indicate something that the person desires (e.g., a drink, a toy, the toilet or help) or to describe something that has been seen or heard (e.g., to join in with a story). Pictures can also be used in daily routines to show something that is happening now or later (e.g., as part of a timetable). This is important for children who do not fully understand the spoken words they hear or who need preparing for an activity. Pictures generally promote independence and, when used correctly, enhance not reduce (spoken) vocabulary. The value of pictures should therefore not be underestimated or overlooked and this is the view taken in the poem. Communication books and timetables – in their various forms – are not items to be stored until needed, or hidden away to prevent damage or loss, they are arguably just as vital as the glasses that help a person see, the inhaler that helps a person breathe or the wheelchair that helps a person move.

How we can help

1. Children often begin by learning just a few pictures but these can quickly accumulate in time. Try creating a folder to store larger numbers of *timetable* pictures and organise these like a day-to-view diary. This makes it easier to find the ones you need at the start of the day or later on, rather than rummaging through a pocketful of them. If children are using large numbers of *communication* pictures, try organising these in a separate book and into categories such as drinks, food, toys, colours and so on.

2. Make sure that timetables and the communication boards/ books are thoughtfully located (i.e., physically accessible in well-defined areas) and have scope to be portable. Children may need to carry them around so that they instantly have the means to understand a routine and to communicate.

3. Encourage flexibility with routines and language by introducing 'surprise' or 'not available' cards. Changes to parts of the day can then be signalled to the child in a planned way and she can have a strategy for requesting something that is not yet symbolised in her book – and understand when something is not available.

Where we can go next

* Jackson, J. (2004) *Multicoloured Mayhem*. London and Philadelphia, PA: Jessica Kingsley Publishers

Jacqui wrote this book as a parent of several children on the spectrum (including her son Luke). Chapter 4 is devoted to autism and has a section on therapies and interventions. She comments on the difference that the Picture Exchange Communication System (PECS)[1] made to her son Ben.

* Roth, I. (2010) *The Autism Spectrum in the 21st Century. Exploring Psychology, Biology and Practice*. London and Philadelphia, PA: Jessica Kingsley Publishers

A readable textbook that explores autism in different fields of endeavour. Section 6.4 discusses various interventions

---

1   The Picture Exchange Communication System (PECS) was created by Andrew Bondy and Lori Frost in the 1990s. It gives children the means of communicating with others and there are six phases. PECS can be used to request activities and is a system separate to that involving timelines, Now and Next boards etc.

for developing language and communication and includes a description of PECS.

43. To Cut a Long Story Short
(A poem about writing and editing)

When
I write
'The End' that
Should mean 'The End'.
Not checking or improving what I've penned.
What have I done wrong? Don't make me amend.
Can't you see that
Change does not
Equal
End?

What we can learn

Children with autism can have an innately rigid view of how the environment, its routines, objects and people should present, and often act in ways that serve to maintain this level of 'perfection'. This desire for perfection reveals itself in many forms, such as persistently adjusting the position of items on a table, eating particular foods in the right order, walking the same route in the garden, choosing the best word for a sentence or worrying about the font on their screen. While these behaviours may look irrational to the casual observer, you can be sure that, for the child, they will have involved an intense measure of concentration. So, when a person intervenes or proposes something different, the child can react with extreme upset or astonishment; writing is a salutary example. Over the years, I have had many conversations with staff about children who find writing difficult (handwriting, punctuation and comprehension) and in particular the process of drafting and editing seems to recur as a popular theme – reminding us how children can quite literally take offence at the idea of 'improving' their work given the effort they have put in. Children with autism like things to be right and right first time. When someone indicates that their work needs to be improved, children may either assume this is a personal failing and a sign of their futility (giving up or destroying their work), or show complete incredulity, unable to see how their work could possibly be any better.

How we can help

1. Develop a culture in the classroom that shows how mistakes are part of everyday life and crucial in the process of learning; you could build a wall display of quotes to this effect, endorsed by popular celebrities (referring to it or the principle regularly). Adults who highlight their own mistakes and treat them in a humorous manner will help children see how they can manage their own in a positive way.

2. Make it clear from the start that the work will be rewritten and state how many times, possibly linking each stage with a concept that is meaningful to the child. For example, if she likes vehicles, try working through a traffic light system such that the final draft is coded red; if she likes LEGO®, use the idea of building a figure (legs, body, head); if she likes gaming, you could use the idea of levels and so on.

3. Teach the process of drafting as a series of steps where specific pieces of information are checked. These can be listed on a pro forma and ticked off when completed, for example

searching for spelling mistakes, ensuring capital letters are used at the start of sentences or replacing adjectives with 'power' words (referring to a spelling board).

Where we can go next

* Attwood, T. (2000) *Asperger's Syndrome*. London and Philadelphia, PA: Jessica Kingsley Publishers. (Original work published in 1998.)

Chapter 6 focuses on children's thinking styles and how these, for example, impact on their memory, their flexibility and their imagination.

* Kluth, P. and Chandler-Olcott, K. (2008) *A Land We Can Share*. Baltimore, MD: Paul H. Brookes Publishing Company

This book explores ways of teaching literacy to pupils on the spectrum and Chapter 6 concentrates on writing skills.

44. A Lesson on Words
(A poem about alien words)

In our class today
We were given a test
To sort real from not real words
Into a bin or treasure chest.

I found it annoying
It made me all tense
The way that I see it
Most words are non-sense.

What we can learn

Have you ever tried to explain the difference between something that is real and something that is not real to a child with autism, or indeed any child? It's inherently difficult! How, for instance, do we know when a person or animal is real if, at any moment, this could be in reference to a picture, book, cartoon, newspaper, advert, the internet, TV soap, film, documentary, YouTube clip, music video, video game or TV/radio programme? It might seem straightforward to begin with, but then when you start to consider the variations, permutations and social nuances involved (entities that may be flat, still, moving, costumed, disguised, invisible or computer generated), you realise how much of our understanding is intuitive and flexible. And if you have accomplished that, how about explaining the difference between real and imaginary entities in the context of language? Perhaps teaching the concept of real versus imaginary to someone who believes a word is a unit consisting of one or more letters that can be pronounced (meaning that *any* word regardless of its spelling is 'real'). Or explaining the concept to someone who believes that nonsense words are those that don't make sense (so *any* word that causes the individual confusion is a 'nonsense' word). Or even suggesting that words without an agreed definition cannot be real (posing problems for those who associate an 'alien' word with a personal interpretation). These are all plausible challenges for people with autism and not the sum of them. Words can also be tricky in the sense of triggers – words that children simply take exception to (because they don't like them); or problematic in view of words they have never seen before (struggling to accept 'new' words).

How we can help

1. Consider whether the explanation of how the words are distinguished is problematic, as changes to this may be beneficial, for example what if the child thinks that words can never be real because her understanding of 'real' is something living and breathing? If the explanation itself is not 'real' and relevant, then the task itself is 'nonsense'...

2. Some children may have to learn the difference between real and nonsense words in a rote fashion to begin with. These words can be memorised by associations that are meaningful to the individual, such as linking them to favourite colours or special interest characters (e.g., all real words are wizards and all nonsense words are spells).

3. Make use of dictionaries where appropriate, such that words can be checked against a definite source (tapping into electronic sources if these are motivating). Children could invent their own dictionaries and create nonsense definitions or characters to go with specific words.

Where we can go next

* Attwood, T. (2015) *The Complete Guide to Asperger's Syndrome.* London and Philadelphia, PA: Jessica Kingsley Publishers. (Original work published in 2007.)

  Chapter 9 looks at children's cognitive abilities and includes a section on problem solving, which Tony refers to as the 'Frank Sinatra Syndrome' or 'My Way' (see p.249).

* Cohen, M.J. and Sloan, D.L. (2007) *Visual Supports for People with Autism.* Bethesda, MD: Woodbine House

Chapter 3 provides examples of visual aids that can be used to support the development of language.

45. Problems with Pronoun
(A poem about pronouns)

Is it you or is it me?
Is it her or is it she?
Is it thee or is it thine?
Is it yours or is it mine?
Is it us or is it we?
Is it him or is it he?
Is it they or is it them?
Confusing language.
Big prob-lem.

What we can learn

In some of my more pedantic moments, I find myself wondering exactly who 'they' are. *They* say that heavy snow is forecast. *They* should have known better. *They* said it was lovely... Of course, I do know who *they* are and, like you, can make a good guess as to the circumstance each pronoun relates to. I've had lots of practice over the years and excusing the odd typo am not generally prone to muddle them. Pronouns can, however, be quite a problem for youngsters on the spectrum – mysterious in their ambiguity and frustrating in their translations and derivatives. A basic mastery of pronouns should develop in a child's early years, perhaps by the age of 4, but can take longer to accomplish with some children. Excepting those who seem to learn 'mine' rather quickly – confusions typically include children who refer to themselves by name in a sentence rather than using 'I' (e.g., *Sarah* wants a biscuit instead of *I* want a biscuit). Others may jumble their shes and hes; some will refer to a person as a thing (e.g., saying *that* one or *this* one instead of you/him/his/her/hers), and still others may misunderstand a communication and echo what someone says (e.g., What's your name? Give it to me).

Children's errors are not unusual in the context of learning language but the longevity or intensity of them is notable in autism; children can become adept at labelling people and objects but find it hard to develop new ways of referring to those same people and objects (e.g., It can only be 'Sarah' – not she or her). When I talk about autism specifics, I note the importance of adults being good role models; it's an uncanny truth that children are often quicker to imitate the words that we don't want them to use. (I'm sure lots of us have been caught out by a child who has repeated something we have muttered in a moment of irritation.) When it comes to giving instructions or asking questions, for instance, how often do you address a question to your child in the manner: 'Does Bobby want the toilet/a drink/a cuddle?' Or tell her: 'Daddy's going to work now' (omitting the pronouns each time). These language models are perfectly understandable – and may be relevant in some circumstances – but when it comes to teaching pronouns, they just might be unhelpful.

How we can help

1. Perhaps the easiest or simplest strategy to employ is one that involves good verbal modelling. Children who are repeatedly exposed to straightforward and uncomplicated examples in the right contexts will be more likely to use them appropriately.

2. Another way we can model the gender-specific pronouns is by labelling pictures with ready-made sentences, or with colour-coded words that the child assembles as a sentence (e.g., He is reading a book; She is climbing a tree).

3. For younger children, songs may be a more practical and kinaesthetic way to practise using pronouns, with actions and music to enhance learning, whereas older children could learn through apps or dedicated software such as *Clicker 7*.

Where we can go next

* Crick Software (2018) *Clicker 7. The Complete Literacy Toolkit.* Northampton, UK: Crick Software Ltd. Accessed on 13/01/18 at www.cricksoft.com/uk/products/clicker/home.aspx

  Clicker 7 is a versatile literacy program that can be used in different ways for different purposes. The website has videos that explain some of its functions to parents and staff in schools.

* www.integratedtreatmentservices.co.uk

  As a teacher many years ago, I remember using The Derbyshire Language Scheme to teach children how to construct sentences and found that colour coding helped with the sequencing of words. It is still used by speech and language therapists today and information about it can be found on the listed link. Another scheme popularly used is called Colourful Semantics and is also explained within the website.

46. What? Where? Why? Who?

(A poem about idioms and metaphors)

What's better than sliced bread?
Who's had Shredded Wheat?
Why do you frighten me with things I can't eat?

Where's the bridge I must cross?
And who's rocked the boat?
If we're going out, I want my green coat.

Why ring a bell?
And who's changed their tune?
If there's lots of noise, I will leave very soon.

Who's hit the nail?
And is built like Fort Knox?
I think it is you with no tools in the box...

What we can learn

My explanation of this poem begins somewhat obscurely with the childhood saying: *Sticks and stones may break my bones but words will never hurt me.* Think about what that would mean to a child on the spectrum – someone who approaches the world in a logical and literal way. It is of course supposed to be a clever remark that a person can use when being teased and – according to Wikipedia (2018) – one that encourages the individual 'to ignore the taunt, to refrain from physical retaliation, and to remain calm and good-natured'. The saying seems apt (or ironic) in a discussion on literalness, idioms and autism. Would a child stay calm and good-natured if our explanation conflicted with her first interpretation? (A stick *can't* break my bones because they are strong and inside my body. Sticks and stones are dangerous. My teacher says I'm not allowed to throw them.) When words don't make sense to us, hurt in the form of confusion and anxiety is a possible consequence. Whether children are verbally fluent or not, metaphors, idioms and sayings can pose real problems for many on the spectrum. Confusing and illogical, they can even cause distress. Imagine the fear prompted by a literal understanding of someone saying, 'You're on fire today' or 'Keep your eyes peeled'. That said, these phrases are unlikely to be the worst offenders. The most difficult ones to deal with are more likely to be the ones that lots of people use lots of the time – 'Go and wash your hands in the toilet', 'Mind your head', 'Watch the road', 'In a tick', 'I'm on the phone', 'In a minute', 'I'll call/text you'. These are everyday phrases that many of us acquire and deliver without even realising, until they're pointed out or someone checks us on them: 'You said you'd call', 'It's been more than a minute'. This literalness means children take things at face value and assume people are speaking in truths (which may account for the indignation in some when they know that the person's statement is a 'lie' – pigs don't fly). In turn, this also means that children struggle to read between the lines of communication or to infer more than one meaning from it, confused by people who say one thing but actually mean something else.

How we can help

1. I'm not suggesting that we avoid using idioms and metaphors with children on the spectrum, but I am suggesting that adults be mindful of the way in which they impart information and colour their language. Know the children who interpret words in literal ways and be proactive in avoiding frustration. Use phrases that you know your child can understand. You don't

use word-heavy instructions with non-verbal children, so why would you use idiom-heavy language if your child has no comprehension of idioms?

2. For older and more verbally fluent children, try setting time aside to talk about popular idioms in a structured way. There are plenty of picture resources and packs available to support your explanations. An investment in time should be beneficial in the long term – decreasing children's anxiety by teaching them how to recognise and use metaphors and idioms for themselves.

3. For children who are continually upset by figures of speech, you could make them playful and profitable, for example encouraging children to spot them in conversations and to record them on pieces of paper that are posted in an 'idiom' box. These could be explained and then exchanged for tokens or pence, which ultimately lead to a reward. (You may want to set some limits so that you don't 'break the bank' so to speak!)

Where we can go next

* Vermeulen, P. (2012) *Autism as Context Blindness*. Shawnee, KS: Autism Asperger Publishing Company (AAPC). (Original work published in 2009.)

Peter explains how context blindness (which I mentioned earlier) has a role to play in the misinterpretation of written and visual information. He discusses the effect of context in communication in Chapter 5, which also includes a piece on the literal understanding of language.

* Welton, J. (2005) *What Did You Say? What Do You Mean?* London and Philadelphia, PA: Jessica Kingsley Publishers. (Original work published in 2004.)

  A helpful book featuring one hundred metaphors, which are humorously illustrated, explained and then exemplified.

Chapter 19

PE

47. Offside Rules
(A poem about football and team games)

Over the top, hopeful and
Free
For a second, unmanned.
Shoot on target, expecting victory,
Irrespective of charging livery.
Disappointment is the poppy-red siren of defeat.
Explanations and endorsements are bittersweet.

What we can learn

While I was drafting this poem on sport, I tried to imagine how a primary school child – influenced by a history lesson on World War I – might experience a game of football. I wanted to capture the idea of someone who loves being outside and adores football but whose interpretation of the rules and interactions with players is not always accurate. As the poem evolved, however, the idea of war struck me as an intriguing metaphor for the 'battles' that autistic children can face with PE or sport (or Sport's Day for that matter). Some children, for instance, love the practical and physical nature of exercise. It contributes to their sensory regulation (feeding the vestibular and proprioceptive systems) and overrides language or learning difficulties, allowing them to perform or compete at the same level as – or higher than – their peers. Children often feel fulfilled by a wider degree of freedom too, moving in larger spaces that are visually clearer and unbounded by long periods of sitting. The rules of sport and the structure of games can also be comforting to children who love order and routines, and implicitly teach them important social skills.

Children who are unmotivated by PE, however, and whose traits are magnified rather than developed through skill training, will quite possibly experience lessons as something akin to my hypothetical 'battlefield'. If we know, for example, that a child has problems with sensory processing, we can imagine how its various manifestations might swiftly lead to avoidant or antagonistic behaviour. The simple act of getting changed could pose a challenge even before the lesson has started, for example in terms of fine motor skills, sequencing and clothing sensitivity (particularly if he has forgotten his kit and is told to wear spare items). These issues might then precede difficulties in the next phase/s of the lesson, such as an inability to cope with trapped or competing sounds (claps, cheers and whistles via the hall, gym, swimming pool or field), to judge personal space, and to coordinate movements. If we add these to the social and linguistic expectations of the lesson for a child who prefers to be alone, finds it difficult to follow instructions and is distressed by losing, then we can be fairly certain that a Great War will ensue.

How we can help

1. While it is common practice to use a visual timetable in lessons, I have discovered that this method is not automatically applied to lessons in PE. Some children will require this – a breakdown shows them what activities to expect, their order

and when the lesson will end. The breakdown is also helpful for children who are impatient to use certain equipment or who associate a place with a particular activity, for example assuming that they will always use the ropes and frames when they enter the gym.

2. Children who find it difficult to navigate open space and areas will likely benefit from extra visual clues that define limits more clearly, such as using tape on the floor to show where the child should stand, cones to indicate where the warm-up occurs or coloured baskets to show where resources are collected and tidied. Special consideration may be needed for flooring that is already marked as standard (e.g., a gym with marked tennis courts).

3. Where children struggle with the social demands of team games, focus on small steps that harness their existing skills, and build on these incrementally. Children could learn to put out or tidy equipment, keep score, referee, be encouraged to join in with particular elements or practise a specific role at length (rather than rotating weekly).

Where we can go next

* Hagerty, F. (2016) 'Star of Pitch and Screen.' *Your Autism Magazine.* Summer edition, 27–30

This article featured an interview with Tom Morgan, a rugby player diagnosed with Asperger syndrome (and other conditions).

* Webster, A. (2016) *Autism, Sport & Physical Activity.* London: The National Autistic Society. Accessed on 02/02/18 at www.

autism.org.uk/products/core-nas-publications/autism-sport-booklet.aspx

You can download this handy booklet from the website, which explains some of the ways in which autism and sport complement and challenge one another and illustrates how issues can be addressed. The foreword was written by Tom Morgan (see previous bullet point).

Chapter 20

PLAYTIME AND BREAK TIME

48. Nursery Times
(A poem about going out to play)

Oh The Grand Old Duke of Talk
He helps me now and then
He marches me out to the school playground
And sings me back again.

And when I am out, I will shout
And when I am in, I will grin
And when I am only half way out
I will cry until I win.

What we can learn

This poem focuses on a young child who prefers to be indoors and gets upset when she is expected to go outside. Perhaps it's because she is sensitive to the cold or is bothered by noise. Maybe she fell over on one occasion and doesn't want this to happen again. Or maybe it is the vastness of the playground with little idea of how to use it that causes the distress. We cannot always know what the problem is, but we can be fairly sure that the reasons are obvious and logical to the individual. In such moments, we can decide whether to accept the child's will or enforce our own, judging whether the behaviour is symptomatic of a tantrum or of genuine anguish. Regardless, if the behaviour recurs, it should be addressed with specific aims and strategies that change how the person understands and copes with the problem. In this instance, we have an adult who knows that the child is motivated by nursery rhymes and prepares her for time outside by singing each of the steps involved.

How we can help

1. Use a portable timeline that prepares the child for going outside and shows her that this event will a) come to an end and b) be followed by something she likes.

2. Identify a particular area or safe space that the person feels comfortable with and practise visiting this at quiet and busy times.

3. Try introducing a special box that is used for outdoor play – a box that contains one or more activities that the child likes. She could choose something to take outside each day and activities could be rotated daily to signal the changes of days in the week.

Where we can go next

* Cumine, V., Dunlop, J. and Stevenson, G. (2010) *Autism in the Early Years*. London: Routledge. (Original work published in 2000.)

   Chapter 8 provides lots of useful information regarding different types of play and how to encourage this.

✱ Elvén, B.H. (2010) *No Fighting, No Biting, No Screaming.* London and Philadelphia, PA: Jessica Kingsley Publishers

Try reading Chapter 5 to appreciate why we need to stay calm in the presence of conflict and to consider possible strategies.

49. The Grate Outdoors
(A poem about sensory play)

The door is opened and I'm free at last
Make for the playground as shadows dance past.
I follow the wall and step over lines
Reaching the corner where sun never shines.
Seeking a space where I'll desaturate
A shelter of sorts, it's my special grate.
I've found a black hole, which swallows up light
Where colours fade out and day becomes night.
Flushing out smells, getting rid of the sound
Carrying them away deep underground.
Everything shakes as I stare through the grill
Waiting for the moment all becomes still.
Scrambled sensations get sucked down the drain
My system reboots and starts up again.

What we can learn

Autism is often described as a 'hidden' disability, quantified by unusual behaviours rather than specific physical features, which are not always immediately visible or apparent. Play (and playtime) provides us with an interesting example given the interests that children may develop and how they spend their time outside: these can be unusual in their type and intensity and unusual considering the person's age and the context. So, we might expect a child who has 'visible' learning difficulties to play with toys geared towards a lower age group, but find it harder to appreciate why another child would, for instance, want to spend hours playing with a blade of grass, or staring into a drain. Whenever I watch children with autism play, I am always fascinated by their ingenuity and their uniquely different perspectives on how we should explore everyday things. And the word 'perspective' is significant. What if the grass that held their attention was instead an iPad or tablet?

How we can help

1. Children with autism need their down time as much as any other person but may satisfy this in ways that are not necessarily typical or expected for their age. If we are sure that the individual is not putting herself or others at risk, then it should be possible to strike a balance between time that is adult-led and time where the child can be true to her (autistic) self.

2. If children are engaging in risky interests, try to find a more viable alternative, which channels or replaces the interest instead of excluding it altogether. In the scenario in the poem, the person could access a pop-up tent, canopy or blanket that defines a quiet space and creates the darkness required. The space could be stocked with a box containing objects that minimise sounds (ear defenders or headphones), neutralise unwanted smells (cloths infused with preferred scents) and occupy restless hands (stress balls, spinners, twiddles).

3. Adults may need to educate the child's peers so that they can understand the person's interest or behaviour and know how to respond positively.

Where we can go next

* Heller, S. (2003) *Too Loud, Too Bright, Too Fast, Too Tight*. New York, NY: HarperCollins Publishers

Another book packed with information and ideas relating to sensory processing.

* Stock Kranowitz, C. (2003) *The Out-of-Sync Child Has Fun. Activities for Kids with Sensory Integration Dysfunction*. New York, NY: The Berkley Publishing Group

This book is also full of ideas that you can use with children who have sensory processing difficulties.

50. You're It
(A poem about winning and losing)

Outside on the yard
Can feel my heart deep inside
It's beating so hard.

Whose turn is it now?
Must be Phillip or Stephen
They're talking in row.

It's Phillip. Damn. RUN!
Cannot get caught. Must not lose
Legs weigh like a ton.

I wasn't tagged. NO!!
It isn't my turn. Not mine.
I wasn't too slow.

It's simply not fair.
Why do they always get me?
It's too much to bear.

What we can learn

When I am outside writing a playground observation, I am struck by how little things have really changed since I was at primary school in the 1980s. Health and safety concerns may have proliferated alongside educational drives, but play persists in a reassuringly familiar way. There are still boys trading cards or girls chatting on benches (and vice versa). Footballs are still being launched across open spaces and bikes bashed into walls and ankles. And children still continue to chase each other in bewildering games, which faintly resemble my British Bulldogs, Off Ground Tick and Stuck in the Mud of old, but that they refer to as Tag. When I watch a game of Tag, I immediately see how confusing and potentially upsetting it must be for a child with autism. Indeed, Tag may well be an acronym for Touch and Go: a sentiment describing the fine line between happiness (not being tagged = winning) and misery (being tagged = failure). This poem portrays the experience of one child who looks forward to the game but becomes anxious once it starts, trying to process the mixture of thoughts and feelings derived from his understanding of the game and the ensuing interactions. We can see how he struggles to keep up with the physical and social pace of the game and, once tagged, interprets this pessimistically – that people 'always' chase him rather than his peers, that he is useless and that the game always ends like this. Failure to children with autism may be experienced as something many times worse than that in others and/or relate to something more obscure or minor – that their disappointment is unexpected, long lasting or disproportionate (getting upset over 'nothing'). They can focus in on a particular detail without grasping the wider social picture (e.g., other people have been tagged) and thus find it hard to change their mindset and their behaviour.

How we can help

1. With the peer group in question, determine what the rules of the game should be from everyone's perspective and summarise those agreed on a poster or rules sheet, which can be displayed in the playground (as a reminder to all).

2. Practise playing the game at quiet times as part of social skills training, and take turns to allocate a 'referee' – someone who can monitor the flow of the game. While this might seem like a heavy investment in time, it may ultimately be labour saving if, for instance, every break time otherwise involves dealing with an incident.

3. A Social Story™ on losing graciously can teach individuals ways of coping with disappointment and frustration where such feelings arise.

Where we can go next

* Al-Ghani, K.I. (2014) *The Disappointment Dragon*. London and Philadelphia, PA: Jessica Kingsley Publishers

  This book comprises four colourful stories illustrating what disappointment can look like and concludes with a section on coping strategies.

* Timmins, S. (2017) *Successful Social Stories™ for School and College Students with Autism. Growing Up with Social Stories ™*. London and Philadelphia, PA: Jessica Kingsley Publishers

Siobhan's book (with a foreword by Carol Gray) provides us with eight stories relating to break time – including one on chasing games – and also has a section on winning and losing.

51. Make or Break Time

(A poem about the difficulty of mixing)

Should
I stand
By myself
Feeling alone?
Or make friends so that I'm not on my own?
Teased either way. Don't know where to begin.
If I do it
Or not, I
Cannot
Win.

What we can learn

The children who love being outdoors relish, I'm sure, the opportunity to move without interruption and to engage in the activities they like the most, whether that means running up and down, playing chase, acting out stories, walking the fences, spinning, using equipment or being with friends. It can be an opportunity to let go of tensions and anxieties that have accumulated in class and to escape social demands if desired. Despite this, break times are potentially fraught with problems such that children can end them feeling worse than before they went out. If you are a person with autism who is absorbed by special interests and prefers to be solitary, then break times may only be stressful when people try to interact with you or encourage you to do something else; adults may feel that children can only be happy when they play with others and are not on their own. But what if you are someone who does want to be with others but doesn't know how to make that happen? Someone who imagines that people think you are 'weird' when you are on your own *and* when you are with them? That even when you try, people don't want to play your games or hear about your interests? That you can never get things right and things always seem to go wrong? This poem highlights the dilemma that children can face during break time and intimates that 'break' in the positive sense of the word could in fact mean something negative – a breakdown.

How we can help

1. Use a Social Story™ to help children know what the options are at break times – teaching them what is available, how to organise themselves and how to get involved. The story may reassure particular individuals that enjoying their own company for periods of time is an acceptable and reasonable thing to do.

2. Work with the child to devise a circle of friends and share this with key adults and other children so that social interactions can be facilitated in a sensitive and meaningful way.

3. A keyring housing a number of conversation starters may be a discrete way of promoting independence, reminding children how they can start an interaction.

Where we can go next

* Carter, M.A. and Santomauro, J. (2010) *Friendly Facts.* Shawnee, KS: Autism Asperger Publishing Company (AAPC)

* Day, P. (2009) *What is Friendship?* London and Philadelphia, PA: Jessica Kingsley Publishers

Both books will give you practical advice on ways of helping children understand, build and sustain friendships. Photocopiable resources are included in the text.

52. OMG

(A poem about masking social skills)

OMG she's at it again.
Going on, on and on
About her MILLION boy-men.

Last week it was Mark and now it is BEN.
To me it is neat
That he's number TEN.

So what if they've made it past the FIRST post.
I've counted SEVEN from here
So that's hardly a boast.

Kissing is stupid. Why do it in French?
I've enough problems with English
On this TWENTY TWELVE bench.

And if Marcie's been cheating, that's breaking a rule.
She'll get ONE HUNDRED lines
From strict Mr Newall.

Still. I'll just nod my head, like I'm all in the know.
And think about NUMBERS
Until the bell goes.

What we can learn

Traditional descriptions of autism state that its incidence is higher in the male population than in the female one – and this certainly resonates with my former teaching years, where the children I taught were predominantly boys. Contemporary research, however, has identified gender differences in the presentation of autism and enabled a greater number of females to be diagnosed – females that historically would have been misdiagnosed because their difficulties were subtler and easier to mask. Girls with autism still have problems communicating and interacting with others but, as we have discussed, seem to learn ways of managing these so that they are less obvious, such as carefully copying mannerisms, phrases or styles of speech in their friends, and enjoying special interests that are less likely to be regarded as unusual (like books, animals or boys). This characteristic type of behaviour, introduced in Part 1, is referred to as masquerading and can prove costly in the sense of people (and the individual) underestimating its long-term impact on mental health. Teenage girls with autism are no different from teenage girls without autism in wanting to develop an identity that is acceptable to themselves and to their peers. They may not understand the complexities of relationships, nor have a specific desire to develop them, but this does not mean they are oblivious to peer pressure and social expectations. This poem exemplifies a situation where an autistic girl is more interested in maths than boyfriends, but pretends otherwise to avoid drawing attention to herself.

How we can help

1. Identify a key person with whom the individual can check in on a regular basis so that worries, concerns or misconceptions can be dealt with systematically.

2. Give the person opportunity to read books about teenage relationships so that she has a factual and objective account of what these may involve, supplementing these with discussion as needed.

3. Where possible and appropriate, encourage participation in break or lunchtime clubs that harness the individual's hobbies, strengths and interests.

Where we can go next

* Hartman, D. (2015) *The Growing Up Guide for Girls*. London and Philadelphia, PA: Jessica Kingsley Publishers

Davida's book has information that will be useful to refer to when talking to girls about emotions, crushes and friends.

* The Students of Limpsfield Grange School and Martin, V. (2015) *M is for Autism*. London and Philadelphia, PA: Jessica Kingsley Publishers

Limpsfield Grange is a school for girls with autism and featured in a television documentary in 2015. In the foreword, the book is described as being written by teenage girls for teenage girls, and the main text focuses on a girl called M who struggles to come to terms with her perceived differences and her eventual diagnosis.

Chapter 21

GROUP SITUATIONS INDOORS

53. Let Me Sit Here
(A poem about seating position)

Let me sit here please
And not by Mary Thompson
Persil® makes me sneeze.

Let me sit here please
I must be by the window
Staring at the trees.

Let me sit here please
Tom Smith has got no shoes on
Smells like mouldy cheese.

Let me sit here please
Can't stand that old projector
Buzzing bumble bees.

Let me sit here please
Otherwise it's difficult
Course. No one believes.

What we can learn

This poem is about a child who feels she can only concentrate and stay calm when she sits in a particular place in class. In this position, she is more able to manage her sensitivity to the sights, smells and noises she experiences. Many children with autism are affected by sensory information in the environment and may avoid or seek stimulation to make themselves feel better. These sensory thresholds and triggers are not always evident to others, and the resulting behaviours can easily be misconstrued as inappropriate, non-functional and disruptive. Typical sensory behaviours may be witnessed as restlessness and frequent movement, hand flapping, tipping on a chair, covering ears, making noises, staring into space or falling silent.

How we can help

1. Complete a sensory audit to determine which aspects of the learning environment support or hinder the child's engagement – inviting her to contribute to this where appropriate.

2. Factor in time for children to have movement breaks to separate periods of sitting and consider resources that may help children concentrate better, such as a task schedule, weighted materials or sensory objects. The task schedule is usually a word list or sequence of pictures that breaks the lesson into bite-sized chunks. Weighted materials are meant to be calming and could include a lap blanket or weighted jacket, while sensory objects could include a wobble cushion, a stretchy toy or an elastic chair band (i.e., a strip placed between the front legs of the chair that offers pressure when she pushes her legs against it).

3. Give the child advance warning if she needs to sit in a different place, explaining the reason why and how long this will be for. Photos and name cards can help children identify the 'correct' places to sit.

Where we can go next

* Smith Myles, B., Tapscott Cook, K., Miller, N.E., Rinner, L. and Robbins, L.A. (2000) *Asperger Syndrome and Sensory Issues*. Shawnee, KS: Autism Asperger Publishing Company (AAPS)

Chapter 3 talks about ways of assessing sensory processing issues and provides a range of example assessment tools – useful for gathering information about a child in an area of need.

* The National Autistic Society (2016) *Visual Supports*. London: The National Autistic Society. Accessed on 04/11/17 at www.autism.org.uk/visualsupports

This webpage explains how visual supports are useful and gives examples of the different types, including task scripts, behaviour cues, emotion thermometers and Social Stories™.

54. Carpet Time
(A poem about participating in groups)

If I know the answer
Why do you shout?
Don't want to forget it.
I have to call out.

If I know the answer
And the others are wrong.
I don't see the point
Of waiting so long.

If I know the answer
You should give me a star.
I've joined in the most
Out of everyone so far.

If I know the answer
Why do I have to be shown?
And why are you surprised
When I want to be on my own?

What we can learn

Carpet time in nurseries and primary schools often involves
children gathering around an adult who leads the group in one
or more structured activities (which vary according to their
purpose and the time of day). Children are expected to listen
to the adult's input and to reply with questions, answers, ideas,
chants, songs or actions – and to know how and when they
should contribute as an individual or with the group. While this
can present challenges for many youngsters, including those
without a diagnosis, it is the autistic child's ability to read and
adapt to a social situation that influences their participation.
Children who are focused on their own agenda and lack a sense
of belonging to a group are more likely to act as if others are
not there, oblivious to the conventions of waiting, taking turns
or sharing, for instance. Children may also perceive the situation
in only one domain, such that they concentrate on a particular
element of the moment and interpret this in a literal way, for
example if an adult asks a question, it should be answered:

questions 'always' need to be answered (and there is only 'one' answer). This poem shows what the difficulties might look like in real terms – where the child listens to the questions, knows all the answers and needs to offer them, and where the child is frustrated by the adult and her peers and does not realise that the converse could equally be true.

How we can help

1. Make the use of picture cards for carpet rules and practical objects for engagement, a permanent or regular feature of teaching.

2. Use a talking stick, teddy, object or named lolly stick (chosen from a pot) to denote the speaker's turn, making it visually clearer to see and track turns.

3. Give the child a mini whiteboard so she can write the answer down while she is waiting (and then show it after another person has answered).

Where we can go next

* Leventhal-Belfer, L. (2008) *Why Do I Have To?* London and Philadelphia, PA: Jessica Kingsley Publishers

   A handy book with stories explaining why children have to do certain things.

* Moyes, R.A. (2004) *Incorporating Social Goals in the Classroom.* London and Philadelphia, PA: Jessica Kingsley Publishers. (Original work published in 2001.)

Chapter 3 consists of a series of lesson plans geared towards positive social behaviours, including perspective taking, non-verbal communication and listening skills.

55. Dinner Time
(A poem about school dining rooms)

Dinner time
Acrid, protracted
Queuing, stewing, overheating
Little chance of eating
Food.

What we can learn

I think it's fair to say that school dining rooms and canteens are mostly busy, noisy and smelly places – to be regarded as either favourable or detestable depending on your (sensory) perspective. Certainly, there is an ebb and flow to the tide of people leaving and arriving; there are a wealth of competing sounds that hang in the air as clouds or rain down on ears; and there are invisible trails of uncountable vapours that suffuse both skin and clothing. Amidst all this, children are meant to file in, line up, sit down and eat – within a set period of time – and to conform to social rules that are as mysterious as they are obvious. This poem portrays the idea of a child who has gone to the dining room and is so overwhelmed by the sensory experience that she is unable to eat.

How we can help

1. Allow the child to be one of the first to enter the dining room so that her perception of sounds and smells develops gradually rather than instantly at full strength (as would be the case for the child who is one of the last). If sensory issues are too pronounced, the individual may be better seated away from the dining room with a small group of familiar children, in a quiet space.

2. You could argue that it is just as important for a dining room to be conducive to eating as it is for a classroom to be conducive to learning, so give some thought to where the child should sit. Some, for example, may prefer being by the door (furthest away from the serving hatch and with easy access for a prompt exit) but others may find this troublesome (due to the door's persistent opening and closing, or the vision of crowds approaching). Some children may like to sit by a window or in the same place (like the end of a bench or table), while others may like to sit facing a wall (with fewer things to look at) or with the wall behind them (more secure).

3. A visual aid at the table may provide the person with a calming focal point, such as a favourite object, a timer that shows them how much time is left, or a timetable that states what they need to do before they go outside.

Where we can go next

* Burns, D.J. (2016) *Do Lemons Have Feathers?* London and Philadelphia, PA: Jessica Kingsley Publishers

  David is an adult with autism and presents a personal account of how this has affected him throughout life. Chapter 3 discusses his school days and includes reference to school dinners.

* Kim, C. (2015) *Nerdy, Shy, and Socially Inappropriate*. London and Philadelphia, PA: Jessica Kingsley Publishers

Chapter 7 looks at a range of sensory behaviours and describes sensitivities in the various sensory systems. You can read about sensitivities to smell, taste and touch in the context of food on pages 111–113.

56. Assembly

(A poem about assemblies)

Friday morning rush
Classes barge past with a push
An adult says 'Shush'.

We sit in long rows
When will this start? No one knows
I pick at my toes.

Sir reads from a book
I think of chickens and cluck
Children laugh and look.

Then pupil awards
Claps for the merits they've scored
Fidgeting. Now bored.

Prayers and then singing
Hands wrapped round my head, clinging
Ears are ringing.

Dismissed at long last
Another assembly past
The relief is vast.

What we can learn

Imagine sitting in a place that is too hot or too cold, surrounded by people who sit, stand, shuffle, breathe, cough, sneeze, call out, chant, laugh and sing at different intervals – and from every corner without giving notice of the intention to do so. Imagine being told to sit still, be quiet and listen for an indeterminate length of time, when you want everyone else to be quiet and are desperate to move to stay calm. Imagine being unable to understand any of the information and procedures that follow, and wondering why you have to endure this situation week in, week out. If you are a person with autism, this is what an assembly might feel like to you. Or it might not. Some children with autism do like assembly: assemblies are usually held on certain days of the week and generally follow a predictable format. They feature periods of calm and allow children to sit quietly without demands being made on them directly, and often celebrate interesting events that hold their attention. But consider the social and sensory nature of assemblies and you will find other children under stress. Assemblies are rarely differentiated for individual needs by virtue of delivering to a group and therefore do not always consider how difficult it is for a person who finds social contact confusing and overwhelming. Moreover, they don't necessarily consider how the content relates to the child's personal perceptions until problems emerge.

How we can help

I. Differentiation is just as important in the hall as it is in the classroom. Think about how the child will access the content and what the main aim will be. Where children are struggling, it may be helpful to consider whether they cope better with one type of assembly over another, for example do they like assemblies celebrating good work or are those the ones that particularly upset them?

2. Be realistic about the length of time the child can manage – this might not be for the entire session and may need to be built up gradually. Try arriving and leaving early – ending on a positive note rather than when the child has reached saturation point.

3. Think about how to make the child comfortable in terms of her seating position, and where she is most likely to focus; consider whether she would prefer to sit on a cushion or chair and if it is better for her to sit at the back or at the front of the room. It may also be useful to think about her proximity to peers, staff, doors, windows, radiators and speakers.

Where we can go next

* Rogers, L. (2013) *Visual Supports for Visual Thinkers*. London and Philadelphia, PA: Jessica Kingsley Publishers

    Look at Chapter 8 for suggested ways of clarifying expectations about different behaviours, for instance the type of visuals we can use to show children what we want them to do. One of the nice things about this book is that it includes a CD of printable resources.

* www.twinkl.co.uk

    You should find lots of useful resources here that could be applied to the assembly context, such as schedules, reward charts, behaviour prompts and communication aids.

Chapter 22

WORKING ONE TO ONE

57. One to One
(A poem about accepting support)

Teaching assistant
Wants to help me with my work
But I'm resistant.

Cannot be skitted
Or have my difficulties
Widely admitted.

What we can learn

One of the typical characteristics of an autism diagnosis is the difficulty seeing a situation from another person's point of view. It would be incorrect, however, to assume that all autistic children are so focused on their own agenda that they are immune to the comments and opinions of their peers. Indeed, in older and more able children, it is often the opposite that is true – that they are extremely sensitive to their peers and will continuously try to hide or mask their difficulties to avoid being seen as 'different'. For these children, any help is a sign of failure and an open door for taunts: their rigid thought processes either prevent them from seeing that they need help and the benefits of being helped, or lead them to assume that adult help will result in people making fun of them. In this poem, the child is aware that she needs support but is fearful of accepting this because of what she perceives will follow – trading success in her work for 'success' among her peers.

How we can help

1. Invite children to rephrase the instructions they have been given at the start of the lesson and summarise the main steps on the board, outlining the key actions required. Teachers could additionally timetable sections of the lesson that promote enquiry with peers and adults in the room, giving individuals 'legitimate' opportunity to ask questions or to seek help.

2. In discussion with the young person, determine a discreet code of communication that she can use to ask for help or to be helped, such as putting a certain colour pen on the table.

3. Teaching assistants allocated to children can be deployed in a variety of ways,[1] which should enable and maximise learning and foster independence not dependence. Where relevant, staff can help to reduce stigma by working with different children, promoting the individual's interactions with others and avoiding the custom of attaching themselves too closely to the child.

---

1   If you are curious about the deployment of teaching assistants, you may be interested in this source: Sharples, J., Webster, R. and Blatchford, P. (2015) *Making Best Use of Teaching Assistants. Guidance Report – March 2015*. London: Education Endowment Foundation. Accessed on 25/02/18 at https://v1.educationendowmentfoundation.org.uk/uploads/pdf/TA_Guidance_Report_Interactive.pdf

Where we can go next

* Beaney, J. and Kershaw, P. (2014) *Autism in the Secondary Classroom*. London: The National Autistic Society

  Chapters 4 and 5 contain photocopiable resources and information relating to curriculum access and the use of visuals.

* Collins-Donnelly, K. (2014) *Banish Your Self-Esteem Thief*. London and Philadelphia, PA: Jessica Kingsley Publishers

  Full of useful explanations and practical ideas helping children understand and improve their self-esteem.

Chapter 23

OWN CLOTHES DAY

58. Fancy Stress
(A poem about non-uniform days)

Own clothes day is never cool
Doesn't feel like we're at school
As if someone's messed with all the rules
Turning children into fools.

Will not change the way I dress
Don't see why or even guess
How different clothes help to impress
All they do is cause me stress.

What we can learn

For all the children who do not like wearing their uniform, there are many who regard it as an essential part of school routine. School is 'not school' if you are wearing your own clothes – own clothes are for home. Children with autism are capable of learning different routines but often develop fixed ideas about certain elements of these, homing in on the detail that they consider the most important in order for things to run their proper course. Adapting to a variation in a routine or generalising a skill, as we have seen, is a characteristic challenge for children on the spectrum. In the matter of the poem opening this piece, we have a child who is baffled by her peers and firmly of the belief that you should always wear a uniform to school (irrespective of special events).

How we can help

1. Consider introducing the non-uniform occasion in activities that precede the actual day – teaching the reasons for the event and preparing the child visually for example using a Social Story™ or timeline.

2. Invite children to dress a favourite teddy or design an outfit for a favourite character if they are uncomfortable coming to school without their uniform.

3. Give children the option of wearing the costume or their own clothes for a specific part of the day, rather than the entire day. Individuals may feel happier knowing that they will get to wear their uniform at some stage.

Where we can go next

* Devine, A. (2016) *Flying Starts for Unique Children*. London and Philadelphia, PA: Jessica Kingsley Publishers

  Chapter 28 talks about different types of events that may cause a child distress and suggests a number of strategies.

* Hoopmann, K. (2017) *All Birds Have Anxiety*. London and Philadelphia, PA: Jessica Kingsley Publishers

  A brilliant visual guide that explains anxiety and how to cope. The pages are illustrated by bird-themed photographs that, in all, should make a difficult subject easier to talk about.

Chapter 24

TEASING AND BULLYING

59. Playing Wiv Ayleeunz
(A poem about playground bullying)

mi Mum sezz i hav ortizm.
i wunder how i cort it.
purhaps sheel giv me meddisan
and maybee that will sort it.

she telzz me that mi jeens
arr lyke Daddeys moor or less.
but hizz arr laybulled Top Man
and myn arr M and S.

growwn ups say that I am speshull
diffrant and yewneek.
wyle orl the littull ayleeunz
cawl mee funnee littull freek.

but mi Mum sezz that wer mooving
coz therz owt ov cowntee spase.
i eemajin therl bee astranorts
at thiss hevvanlee playse.

so im preeparing for arr jernee

flying daylee on the yarrd.
dojjing rokks and seeing starz
wen the ayleeunz cum and hit me harrd.

What we can learn

It is rare for me to encounter situations where an autistic child has been bullied. Many of the schools I work with frequently recount examples of children supported by peers who admire their individuality, are caring, fiercely loyal or just happy to be their friend. Predictably, there are always terrible exceptions, often where there is a lack of understanding about the condition and a lack of appropriate structures in place that would otherwise promptly detect and manage, or prevent and deter, incidences. Bullying in any context is a damaging behaviour but particularly detrimental in the context of autism due to the ways in which the person processes social interactions. Children can be vulnerable because they – like the person in this poem – do not realise that they are being treated badly or do not know how to communicate the need for help. Communication difficulties can be many and varied, such that the person doesn't think to ask for help, their abilities significantly reduce in the presence of stress, they react with physical aggression, shut out the problems for fear of recrimination, or begin to view all interactions with others as potentially harmful and therefore as situations to avoid. The child's perspective on bullying can be further exacerbated by occasions where they assume intent when there is none (e.g., when a person looks at them in a certain way or makes an 'innocuous' comment), or when they dwell on incidents long after these have been dealt with.

How we can help

1. Promote awareness of autism throughout the school to improve understanding of the condition and its impact on the person, emphasising the person first. Children should learn that autism is not something to be feared or ridiculed, but something that is part of an individual who should be accepted and respected.

2. Establish a firm code of conduct that guides pupil behaviour in all aspects of school life, supporting positive interactions and promoting emotional wellbeing. In the playground, this may include a list of rules that remind children how to get along with one other, and the creation of playground monitors who help those in need.

3. Cue cards on keyrings are handy memory aids for children who find it difficult to be assertive, to ask for help, or to know how to react at different times. Cue cards can be personalised and may comprise useful phrases or specific strategies. This strategy may be embedded in a larger piece of work that teaches children how to recognise instances of bullying (versus moments of conflict or misunderstanding).

Where we can go next

* Jackson, L. (2004) *Freaks, Geeks and Asperger Syndrome*. London and Philadelphia, PA: Jessica Kingsley Publishers. (Original work published in 2002.)

   In Chapter 10, Luke discusses his own experiences and definitions of bullying.

* https://theplaydoctors.co.uk

A brilliant website for purchasing all manner of visual aids, including communication fans. The range includes aids related to bullying.

60. Riding the Bus
(A poem about bullying out of school)

The bell has gone for the end of the day
I queue for the bus and wait at the door
Count out one fare – though it's twice I will pay:
A trial by journey I must endure.

Shut down, transporting myself far away
As ever, they tip my bag on the floor
Internal thoughts are so hard to convey
Their mindless antics I try to ignore.

Plastic bottles hit my shoulder and head
Laughter snowballs, raining chills down my spine
But they will not win or earn their street cred
The victory lap will always be mine.

Whatever they do I won't make a fuss
Dignity's my prize when leaving the bus.

What we can learn

Having just touched on the problem of bullying in the playground, here we have a poem suggesting how bullying might occur with a secondary pupil on his way home. In both instances, we can see how children with autism are more vulnerable to bullying during unstructured times and when adults are not immediately available. Bullying is a difficult issue to deal with in any circumstance, but will be more pronounced for those students who are unable to share their problems and do not want the extra attention this would invite. They may also assume that this is just how things are and always will be, that they 'deserve' this type of treatment and that no one can help them anyway – suppositions that are naturally very wrong and worryingly indicative of low levels of self-esteem and social understanding.

An additional challenge relates to adults being able to recognise that a person with autism is being bullied when he won't communicate this. How can people help if they do not know? Essentially, we should be vigilant to changes in behaviour, whether these are subtle or marked, for example noticing whether children are suddenly more insistent in their interests and routines, or intent on creating new ones (trying to create some semblance of control). We should notice changes in mood too, for instance children seeming to reach saturation levels of tolerance very rapidly (reacting more intensely or getting upset by things that wouldn't normally bother them). We should also notice children who are quieter or more withdrawn, children who uncharacteristically begin to avoid certain situations, and children whose attendance and punctuality starts to deteriorate (avoiding or being late for school, truanting or delaying their departure at the end of the day). We should notice children who are more visibly anxious than usual or seem more lethargic and less motivated in their work (potentially losing sleep and not eating). These symptoms will not be unfamiliar to those mindful of concerns relating to child protection.

How we can help

1. Ensure that the school's anti-bullying policy clearly states the need for every person to respect every individual at all times,

including time out of lessons, in the playground, travelling to and from school and during clubs. 'Wrap around care' in the *practical* sense should be interpreted literally in the *moral* sense. In secondary school settings, students should be more aware of their moral obligations and understand how these contribute to their community and our society at large – mindful of the laws and legislation that serve to protect us.

2. Apart from the obvious need to address the protagonists, the person being bullied could be coached through a plan of action that teaches appropriate ways of responding – showing that different options are available, that he can take ownership of these and therefore does not have to be a passive recipient.

3. It may help to identify a bus buddy, someone who can act as a direct source of moral support for the individual, or raise awareness of issues if they arise.

Where we can go next

* Gray, C. (2010) *The New Social Story*™ *Book*. Arlington, TX: Future Horizons

Nine of the stories contained within this book are devoted to bullying.

* Stobart, A. (2009) *Bullying and Autism Spectrum Disorders. A Guide for School Staff*. London: The National Autistic Society

This booklet is available as a download online. It clarifies bullying in the context of autism and shows how to promote awareness in schools. Strategies are explained in terms of supporting pupils and tackling incidents.

PART 3

AT HOME

For families living with autism, there really is no place like home, but what it looks like or how it is used will vary from one household to the next. Home may be just as much a refuge from the social, emotional and physical demands of school or work as a battleground for ordinary routine tasks that are experienced as daily ordeals. And though we could easily observe these patterns in a wide range of family units, I'd say that autism in families presents some very unique, distinctive and often 'humorous' challenges. Jacqui Jackson, for instance, is an author and parent of several children on the spectrum and describes her family as 'full of fun and laughter, trials and tribulations, chaos and catastrophes' (Jackson 2004, p.18), before adding, 'Parenting in itself is no easy task, but when you have adolescents, pre-adolescents and many shades of the autistic spectrum all under one roof, then life can certainly be…colourful!' (p.19).

Conversations with parents of children with autism are always fascinating and are indeed colourful. If family life was an autism job advert, it would probably state that 'impatient and inflexible candidates need not apply'. I am continually being educated about the rules, routines and boundaries governing family life and these are not always conventional, and neither is the will of the parents. Over the years, I have learned that food should be served white and in a particular place; that the toilet is a spot in the garden and not in the bathroom; that the television should be watched upside down or 10cm from the screen; that hair can never be cut; that a visitor (like me) should be dealt with by being sat on; that the washing machine is entertaining; and that – under no circumstances – should the house be left to go to the supermarket. Sound familiar to anyone? I'd be surprised if you said 'no'. Whether you have experienced these things or not, there is a point to be made: autism and family life can be amusing and joyous, but are definitely not always easy. Habits that are fondly remembered with nostalgia probably won't have passed without serious difficulty and upset. Imagine trying to teach children to accept an alternative if they have a significant learning difficulty or limited communication skills, or if they find it hard to take on someone else's views or feelings – and when you've only had two hours' sleep, are late for work and your child is in 'meltdown'. It's little wonder that families seek help and are frustrated by the scarcity of resources and services available. But...perhaps things are improving. I'd certainly like to believe that parent voices and voices from the spectrum are getting louder, and that their struggles and successes are being more widely understood and acted on. Life at home can be fun *and* tough; I hope that some semblance of this is captured in the final 33 poems.

Chapter 25

GROWING UP ISSUES

61. Time to Think
(A poem about processing time)

*The last thing I need when I get home from school, is you
hanging around me, pretending we're cool.
I know that you love me and you're just being kind, but
all that I want is the chance to unwind.
Remember my day has been full of demands, so I'm
feeling
as stretched as a taut rubber band.
I need space on my own
And time to relax,
Don't want confrontation or to panic attack.
We can talk later on and swap tales from the day,
When I've had time to think, I'll have much more to say.*

What we can learn

If your day has been stressful and you are thinking about the
things that need to be done or must be achieved by the end of
the evening, do you want to talk about your working day as soon
as you get in? Notwithstanding time with our children, surely
most of us would rather have a cuppa, a sit down with the news
or paper, or to get on with the chores. Children with autism can

experience school in much the same way as you experience work; they need opportunities to 'park' conversations about their day until they're ready and they have had time to process or unwind. It's a great and natural temptation for many families, however, to want to talk about school as soon as they see their child, either at the gate, on the way home or as soon as they get in – even though these are precisely the moments that children are often feeling the most stressed. To talk about school is potentially the last thing they want to do at that time. Indeed, I've had plenty of conversations with parents struggling to deal with upset and frustration at the end of school and discovered a common denominator – namely children who have been expected to relay the day's events before they've had time to settle. It's not an exact scenario for every child and family of course, but it may be something to consider if your child is typically frustrated or ill-tempered during the transition from school day to home time. You may also want to consider whether your child is able to talk about school in the first instance and if she understands the purpose of the conversation, as these factors may account for her apparent refusal to talk about the day, the lack of volunteered information or her standard issue responses. Her reticence on the subject of school could also be attributed to her opinion that you only talk about school at school, or to her belief that 'you' automatically know what she has done because *she* knows.

How we can help

1. Try to keep conversations about the school day to times when you know your child is relaxed, giving her time to settle into the afternoon or evening first. The immediate conversations held at the school gate or the front door may be minimal, perhaps consisting of only a few words that are based on her comments, her interests or the next part of the day.

2. Children may find it easier to transition from school to home if there are particular routines in place to bridge this time – patterns that help them know what to expect as soon as they leave the school building, as they travel home and once they have arrived. These might include: having or avoiding certain conversations at key points, following particular routes, having time to themselves or time with a preferred activity.

3. At the appropriate time, you can help your child share positive aspects of the school day by choosing your questions carefully and using visuals to remind her what she has done. If you know she is finding school hard, you must expect that a simple question such as 'How was your day?' will be met unfavourably and trigger an outburst. You might also want to phrase questions as specific statements (e.g., 'Tell me one game you played at break today') or to ask similar sorts of questions over a period of time, helping her predict what information will be required.

Where we can go next

* Dyrbjerg, P. and Vedel, M. (2007) *Everyday Education*. London and Philadelphia, PA: Jessica Kingsley Publishers. (Original work published in 2002.)

This book serves as a great example for parents wanting to introduce visual aids at home, illustrating how this can be done in different areas.

* Verdick, E. and Reeve, E. (2012) *The Survival Guide for Kids with Autism Spectrum Disorders*. Minneapolis, MN: Free Spirit Publishing

Chapter 11 helps us understand some of the difficulties that children experience, and can inform ways of teaching conversation skills.

62. The 'H' Word
(A poem about homework)

Why
Do my
Teachers keep
Giving me work
To do at home if it sends me berserk?
Don't understand it. Makes no sense at all.
I just end up
Throwing it
At the
Wall.

What we can learn

Homework can be a source of conflict for children of all ages with or without a diagnosis of autism, and I think many of us would sympathise with tired and overwrought children who, despite dealing with a day of social and subject-loaded demands, are still expected to revisit or extend their learning through work at home. Children with autism who find homework especially difficult may do so for a number of reasons – not only because their tiredness is compounded by hidden degrees of social effort, but because of their ability to understand its purpose, their ability to organise themselves and their tendency to view situations in black and white. Some, for instance, may believe that school work should only be done at school, that the home environment is completely separate. They may also experience tension in prioritising their wants and needs over external demands, being more interested in satisfying their own wishes and regarding homework as an unwelcome intrusion.

Homework issues, however, are not just a matter of 'reluctance'. They can also comprise problems with organisation and concentration. In the first instance, you might observe a child struggling to collect what she needs for the task and having difficulties knowing where to begin and processing what needs to be done. At other times, you might notice how hard it is for a child to concentrate on her work until it is finished or, conversely, how much energy she puts into this (not necessarily attending to the most salient parts). Clearly, an innate propensity for persistence is not always advantageous. It's little wonder that I often hear parents talking about the hours that their child spends trying to do their homework and about the hours they spend dealing with the frustration it produces.

How we can help

1. Establish a place in the house (dining room, office, bedroom, conservatory etc.) that is consistently homework friendly – conducive to and associated with independent working. Consider the lighting, temperature, decor (busy or plain), potential distractions, seating arrangements and background noise, helping your child to feel at her most comfortable. Other family members may need special instruction to avoid interrupting her while she is working!

2. Schedule homework to particular times of the week so that this becomes a routine part of family life. Decide when your child is most likely to be at her best. Try bookending homework with personal and relaxing time beforehand

and afterwards, and perhaps link homework to a reward or reward system.

3. Use visual aids to help children organise themselves for tasks, for example using timers for pace, writing lists of things they need to collect or do, highlighting key words, and using colour coding or a traffic light coding system for questions.

Where we can go next

* Canavan, C. (2015) *Supporting Pupils on the Autism Spectrum in Secondary Schools.* London: Routledge

  This book has lots of resources to help teenagers organise their written work. Chapter 9 makes reference to a child whose struggles with planning and organisation lead to anger. Management tips are provided.

* Timmins, S. (2017) *Successful Social Stories™ for School and College Students with Autism. Growing Up with Social Stories™.* London and Philadelphia, PA: Jessica Kingsley Publishers

  One of the useful things about this book is that the Social Stories™ are accompanied by explanations for the behaviours they address. Two good examples of this are in the sections on homework and revision.

63. Face Time
(A poem about mobile phones and texting)

I'd
Rather
Stay in my

Room than go out.
It's easier inside, of that there's no doubt.
I'm illiterate with social unknown,
But better with
Messages
On my
Phone.

What we can learn

Many years ago, I remember watching a whole-school assembly during my final year of teaching practice. Each class took turns to perform in front of the audience and I was struck by the difference between children lower down the school and children at the top end. The younger children were bolder and louder; the older children were less certain and more easily embarrassed. It was noticeable but not surprising. We expect children to become more self-conscious as they get older, and, more profoundly, to experiment with the thoughts, values and beliefs that will shape their adolescent identity. We also expect children to seek more time with their peers and to avoid or even challenge adults more, for example being out when they can or retreating to their room when they can't. These habits may similarly develop in people with autism – autism doesn't stop puberty and adolescence – but their manifestation may be more striking, more affective, or interpreted differently.

In many instances, we may come across children on the spectrum who do the reverse of their non-autistic peers, in the sense that they associate less with their peers and spend *more* time with adults (because adults offer predictability, support, tolerance and security). In other instances, we have children on the spectrum who do want to have friends but struggle with the nuances of interactions and discover ways of using technology as a protective screen or go-between. Text messages, for instance, make conversations more structured, breaking them down into sections that can be processed more slowly, in peace, and without the confusion of facial expressions, tone or gestures. While texting is just as problematic as a conversation – find me someone who hasn't felt mildly offended by at least one text they've read in the past – it does at least provide opportunity to judge your turn, to think about what you want to say and to choose when to reply. And all of this with the less immediate social risks of the person tutting in disapproval, laughing or frowning back. In this instance, the teenager knows that she can read written communication (messages) but not communications delivered in social contexts.

How we can help

1. If you are trying to persuade your child to leave her room and interact with others, think about the best time to do this. We already know that it probably won't be straight after school. Be vigilant as to the length of time she is alone in her room, however, because this will affect her willingness to engage with others. The longer the time, the easier it is for her to become engrossed in something she won't leave. Anticipate that she may find the arrangement frustrating at first and compose your response with smiles and reassurance rather than stern looks and a disapproving tone.

2. Interactions with family members will be more explicit if a household rule is introduced and embedded in a predictable routine that involves people spending time together. Identify an activity and agree the time that she spends with you or at least one family member on a regular basis. Ensure that the

activity is of interest to her and consider what your roles will be. If the activity is having tea together, for instance, is this in the dining room or lounge? Will she be expected to chat or just to eat? If the activity is watching TV, will this mean a short programme or will she have to last the length of a film? If you think this sounds formal, it might need to be. It will be easier for her to deal with specific instructions than unspoken expectations.

3. Try organising short mate-dates, identifying peers from your extended family, the school community or the neighbourhood where appropriate. Plan these meet-ups in advance and with consideration of activity, time span and expectation (as above). If your child is known to 'compartmentalise', you may need to explain why she 'has to' interact with a school friend at home.

Where we can go next

* Kutscher, M.L. (2017) *Digital Kids*. London and Philadelphia, PA: Jessica Kingsley Publishers

Try using Chapter 5 as a starting point for setting up rules regarding the use of technology or screen time. The chapter identifies key items to consider, potential rules and opportunities for negotiation.

* Simone, R. (2010) *Aspergirls*. London and Philadelphia, PA: Jessica Kingsley Publishers

Chapters 6 and 9 are of particular note in this context because they address identity and friendships.

64. Smelling Bad
(A poem about hygiene and showering)

They say I should shower to keep myself clean
Apparently, it's a rule
For observing hygiene.

They say I'll look handsome if I shave and I preen
Apparently, it's expected
When you get to your teens.

But how can I shower if my nose is so keen?
My smell masks their smell,
Which I think is obscene.

What we can learn

For those of you with a teenager in the house, personal hygiene is likely to have entered one or more of your conversations at some point, quite possibly in reference to an untidy bedroom with dirty plates and laundry, unwashed or unkempt hair, stale smells or pungent aftershave, compulsive washing or the bathroom queue. Such behaviours will not be unfamiliar to you, nor be thought of as unusual or unexpected. In most cases, however, they will probably be carried out with a level of intention and understanding – with your son or daughter 'choosing' how to act. Teenagers with autism may also exhibit these behaviours but are not as likely to appreciate or be concerned by how they affect other people. Their motivations will probably be different too. In this poem, for instance, we have a teenager who does not want to shower because he can't cope with the smell of shampoo and shower gel. His natural body odour is more familiar and helps to mask the smell of toiletries worn by other people. The fact that showering is a social convention and that people generally dislike body odour is not yet understood or recognised by this youngster. Such differences of opinion (i.e., where teens believe they are acting appropriately without understanding why they are not) can inevitably cause friction and recur in different contexts, for example the teen who equates a tidy room with one where everything (she feels) is in its rightful place; the teen who doesn't wash her hair because she doesn't like the feel of water on her head; the teen who spends an age in the bathroom because he has difficulty with sequencing; or the teen who won't 'suddenly' use deodorant because he hasn't used it in the past. Fortunately, there are lots of ways in which we can help children understand and manage their personal hygiene, and these will be most effective when we remember that we are dealing with two aspects here, not one – teenage behaviour *and* autism. We cannot expect children to conform because we have already told them 'a million times' or that they have come of age.

How we can help

1. Task schedules are advantageous in many ways as they list the steps involved in completing a particular activity and promote the individual's independence. These lists can be presented as words, pictures or symbols and may be short or long depending on the need. They can be laminated on paper, stored on a portable keyring, entered into a diary or calendar, or stored as reminders on a smartphone. Children should be taught how to use them and their use should be monitored in the early stages, allowing the child time to absorb and remember the information. The schedules should be located in an agreed and relevant place (not somewhere easily forgotten or inaccessible) and could be written for all manner of scenarios, such as organising clean and dirty

clothes, using deodorant, or remembering when to shower, bathe or shave.

2. For older children or teenagers, strategies may be more effective if they are determined by the youngster him/ herself through the solution-focused approach I mentioned earlier. In this instance, let's say that one hygiene option is to 'never have a shower'. The advantage of this choice becomes 'I won't have to deal with the smell of toiletries'. However, a disadvantage could be worked out as 'My body may develop a rash, which could become itchy and infected'.

3. Young children will evidently need help to wash because of their age. If your child refuses to wash, say, in the bath, consider not only the obvious sensory processing difficulties regarding the feel of the water and the smell of the soap, but also any proprioceptive and visual processing problems, such as those relating to the depth of the bath, and the contrast between the colour of the water and the unit itself. In this latter regard, you could introduce a step and ensure that the water is coloured.

Where we can go next

* Hartman, D. (2015) *The Growing Up Guide for Boys.* London and Philadelphia, PA: Jessica Kingsley Publishers

Designed for boys aged 9–14, Davida's book helps boys understand different aspects of puberty through a series of illustrated topics. The book includes sections on personal hygiene.

* Musgrave, F. (2017) *The Asperger Teen's Toolkit.* London and Philadelphia, PA: Jessica Kingsley Publishers

This useful teen-based book has important advice relating to relationships and wellbeing.

65. Not Now, Jonathan
(A poem about masturbation)

I have to now, why must I wait?
Why must there be this great debate?
When the pressure's on, I'm in a state
Yet all you do is castigate.

I have to now, why obviate?
Why must you stop me feeling great?
The tension's hard. Not thinking straight
Yet all you do is agitate.

I have to now, not after eight
Can't understand why you're irate.
It's me who's feeling all sensate
Just leave me be to hands of fate.

What we can learn

Our imaginary Jonathan is a teenager who has recently discovered the pleasure of masturbation. Unfortunately, he has not yet learned when and where this is considered appropriate, and tries to fulfil the urge whenever the sensation is triggered. This leads to conflict, with the adult desperately trying to explain that it's not socially acceptable in public (for public, read the classroom, school playground, library, bus queue, cinema etc.), and causes frustration in both senses of the word. The subject of masturbation is always a sensitive one. It is potentially awkward to discuss with any youngster but certainly requires more thought when talking to a person with autism. It's not just about language difficulties, emotional regulation, social interactions, inflexibility and sensory processing; it's also about the ways that children with autism interpret the world around them. We have to understand this in a number of domains if we are to teach appropriate behaviours. We have to understand, for instance, why a child fails to recognise someone's embarrassment when he tries to masturbate in public (not seeing the situation from someone else's point of view), why a child insists on doing it wherever he feels like it (losing sight of the bigger picture), why he tries to masturbate whenever he wants (struggling to control impulses and delay gratification) and why he assumes it is acceptable to do it in public (the problem of generalising). When teaching new behaviours, it is also necessary to consider the motivation and the opportunity for it. Sometimes a behaviour that looks like a child touching his or her private parts, for example rubbing against or on something, can have more to do with a lack of general stimulation than a sexual need. Although this is more typical in the early years than in adolescence, it could factor into responses and interventions at any age.

How we can help

1. If the behaviour is happening on a regular basis, it may be worthwhile keeping a note of when your child engages in the behaviour, how it is triggered and where it occurs. This will help adults be more objective and sensitive in their response and potentially determine whether the behaviour stems from a sensory need or a sexual one. In some cases, this may mean introducing more structure and alternative sensory stimulation, but in others, it could involve teaching the difference between public and private behaviour.

2. For young children who like to rub themselves or press against surfaces in a repetitive way, think of a simple word you can use to interrupt what they are doing and then channel the behaviour into something more functional. You may, for example, sign and say the word 'Finished' and then offer an alternative activity that applies deep pressure, keeps their hands busy or their whole body moving, such as providing a blanket they can wrap around themselves, covering their lap with a weighted pad, making fidget items and pliable objects available, or directing them to indoor or outdoor equipment.

3. For older children and adolescents, Social Stories™ and 'growing up' books are helpful resources as they can explain a delicate subject like masturbation in clear and impartial language. In the right circumstances, stories should provide children with a healthy understanding of the behaviour, equip them with an appropriate vocabulary and teach them when and where the behaviour is deemed acceptable. The stories also provide adults with a consistent narrative and a consistent strategy.

Where we can go next

* Hartman, D. (2014) *Sexuality and Relationship Education for Children and Adolescents with Autism Spectrum Disorders.* London and Philadelphia, PA: Jessica Kingsley Publishers

  Divided into four parts, this book offers parents and professionals a means of explaining a wide range of issues relating to sexuality and relationship education. Social Stories™ are available as resources throughout, and include some relating to masturbation.

* Reynolds, K.E. (2014) *Things Tom Likes*. London and Philadelphia, PA: Jessica Kingsley Publishers

This concise little book deals with the subject of masturbation and is available from the same author as a version for girls (*Things Ellie Likes*). In the manner of a Social Story™, it can be used to teach boys about masturbation and to explain where this is socially appropriate. The pictures are presented as (realistic) cartoon drawings.

66. Cutting Remarks and Salon Reflections

(A poem about haircuts)

Hiyah Big Ben, nice to see you today.
Let's have your coat. Come. Come this way.

> *I can't look at your eyes, or greet you today.*
> *I like wearing my coat, it's a shame I don't say.*

Can you fasten your cloak and sit down on that chair?
Now put your head back, so I can shampoo your hair.

> *I struggle with black and the height of this chair.*
> *My head cannot deal with that fluorescent tube glare.*

How does that feel? Is it too hot or too cold?
Do you want our conditioner? It's hairdressing gold!

> *You think this is hot. I think it's too cold.*
> *My neck has gone stiff, yet I do as I'm told.*

Straighten up now, so I can do the towel wrap.
Let's move to the mirror, there's a good chap.

I am sitting straight. Wish you'd tighten that wrap.
These reflections are painful, but still you must yap.

I'll just get the dryer and give it a blast.
How's things at school? You're growing so fast.

> *The noise of your dryer is like a nuclear blast.*
> *I'm planning my exit while you talk way too fast.*

When's your school holiday? I can never tell.
We're off to France in November. Do you want wax or
some gel?

> *My distress must be obvious. Why on earth can't you*
> *tell?*
> *I'm now incapable of deciding or caring about gel.*

Here is your coat. Is mum paying by card?
Take care of yourself. Don't study too hard.

> *Thank God you have finished. Mum hurry with that*
> *card.*
> *I've got to leave NOW. My heart's thumping me hard.*

What we can learn

It would be an understatement to say that I don't like having my hair cut. I don't remember it being an issue as a girl but it is one as an adult. I'm not going to have a tantrum or refuse to go when the time comes but I also won't enjoy it. I think the discomfort has grown as I've got older because there is a greater expectation of reciprocal conversation in adulthood, and because conversations often comprise questions that I'd rather avoid. I don't want to talk about my plans for the day (as I might be struggling to make them) and I don't want to talk about what I'm doing in the evening (because reading will sound weird). So a trip to the hairdressers generally becomes a contest of competing tensions where I am faced with the choice of remaining silent so that my answers can't 'give me away' or to answer those questions, feel very uncomfortable and still 'give myself away'.

Over the years, I have also started to struggle with the sensory aspects of having my hair cut – though mine are relatively minor compared with those experienced by children. Parents often report their child's issues as those relating to the sound and feel of the scissors or clippers, to the feel of hair falling on skin, or to the worry that hair is being lost. They also talk about children refusing to sit in a high chair or to wear a cape (disliking the sleeves, the colour or texture). Children may not like to have their hair wet or washed or to have someone touch their head. They may not like the sound of the hairdryer or the sound of music and conversation around them. Other children may have issues with sitting still for more than a few seconds and therefore roam the room looking for somewhere to climb, or for (potentially unsafe) items of interest like sockets, wires and toiletries. Older children may simply refuse to have their hair cut because they don't understand why they should or because they have previously been upset by how it turned out.

How we can help

1. Try to arrange haircuts on a *regular* basis so that the actual process is as quick as it can be; the longer you leave the haircut, the longer the hair will be and the longer it will take to cut. Little and often is a useful maxim and means that children have more frequent opportunity to experience their hair being cut. While this may present more stress in the beginning, with the right support, the stress should reduce once the process becomes more routine.

2. To desensitise or prepare your child for her hair being cut, you could practise visiting the salon and exploring the room without the pressure of an actual cut. A sensory diet before and after the visit may be additionally helpful. If her attention allows, she could also watch you or someone else having a haircut to help her know what to expect. Using the same salon and hairdresser will serve everyone in terms of building rapport. If you are very fortunate, the hairdresser may be someone who works privately and can visit at home too (building up to a salon visit).

3. Younger children may benefit from play scenarios that open up ideas as to the things that are involved and how situations occur. This should make the process more fun and easier to understand. Play also gives children opportunities to control what is happening by making choices, and these could be transferred to the salon, for example the colour of the towel, the chair that is used, the cape they will wear.

Where we can go next

* Attwood, T. (2015) *The Complete Guide to Asperger's Syndrome.* London and Philadelphia, PA: Jessica Kingsley Publishers. (Original work published in 2007.)

 You can read more about sensory sensitivities in Chapter 11 of this book. One of the sub-sections refers to tactile sensitivity and includes two paragraphs on haircuts, plus a personal quote from an adult on the spectrum.

* Clements, J. and Zarkowska, E. (2004) *Behavioural Concerns and Autistic Spectrum Disorders.* London and Philadelphia, PA: Jessica Kingsley Publishers. (Original work published in 2000.)

Chapter 9 explores the relationship between sensitivities and behaviour and provides readers with tips and hints for building tolerance.

Chapter 26

FOOD AND DRINK

67. The Blue Bottle
(A poem about new bottles and cups)

I don't want to drink, I just want to chew

    chew

On my favourite bottle that's Thomas blue

    blue

It tastes much better when it's old and not new

    new

Please don't replace it, because I will not thank

    you.

What we can learn

Why do many of us have a favourite mug, one we always reach for among the others in the cupboard or amid the washing up on the draining board? Is it the style or size that lures us? Does it prompt a particular memory of where it was bought or who it came from? Is it something we use on special occasions or on a regular basis? Would we get upset if it was broken and had to be replaced? Or if it wasn't a mug, what about an item of clothing, a favourite book or some footwear? People without autism are just as likely as people on the spectrum to have a favourite item that is personally prized. The difference of course lies within the way that the individual understands and uses the object in a social context. Over the years, I have seen a number of children latch on to a favourite bottle and seem unable to move on to a new one when the time comes, either because the existing one is dirty, damaged or missing, or because they have developmentally outgrown it. While it makes sense to one child that she is now a 'big girl' and can drink from a cup, this piece of information may lack meaning for a child with autism. Children might regard the bottle as the only item that means 'drink' (and thus reject any other vessel) or prefer the bottle to a cup because the chewable stopper is the most important part (that attention to detail again). Children may also struggle to accept something new simply because it's different – symptomatic of a confusing change in routine. The poem above concerns a child who uses her bottle as a chewing toy that soothes and calms her. To change the bottle because it is damaged or because she needs to learn how to drink from a cup is to metaphorically change her levels of anxiety from half empty to half full.

How we can help

1. There are lots of sensory resources on the market that can be used as 'chews', available in different colours, shapes, sizes and textures. Some are chosen to imitate a real-life object (such as a remote control), while others can be held in the hand or worn as a bracelet or necklace. If you invest in a chew and introduce this to your child, make sure you consider aspects of safety, supervision, age, understanding and robustness. Chews are not infinitely indestructible but can be very effective when used appropriately.

2. The chew may need to be introduced gradually, for example by placing it in her line of sight until she is used to it being around and wants to explore. Remember that it will be a 'new' object with a 'new' taste and a 'new' feel and therefore something that needs to be got used to; persistence may be required when teaching her to use it.

3. When teaching your child to move on from a bottle to a cup, you may need to use a similar process of acclimatisation, presenting it intermittently and persistently. Children may be more motivated if their efforts (looking, holding, touching etc.) are rewarded (with smiles, tickles, stickers or songs etc.) rather than criticised.

Where we can go next

* Koscinski, C. (2016) *The Parent's Guide to Occupational Therapy for Autism and Other Special Needs*. London and Philadelphia, PA: Jessica Kingsley Publishers. (Original work published in 2013.)

   Chapter 3 describes ways of developing muscles in the mouth – aiding eating and drinking – and answers some common questions. At the end of the book there are some useful developmental checklists, which span the ages of 2 months to 5 years.

* www.chewigem.co.uk

   One of the many sensory resources websites that can be found on the internet.

68. Today's Lunch is a Set Menu

(A poem about restricted diets)

When you're making my lunch
You better be sure
That you've remembered digestives
And counted out four.

You can quarter my banana
As long as it's raw
But I need two chicken nuggets
Halved once and no more.

As for my chocolate
Perfection is law
If you break that big KitKat®
I'll retch on the floor.

What we can learn

Autistic or not, we all have our own preferences regarding food, whether it's a favourite restaurant or a spot on the sofa, a style of cuisine, a method of cooking or that essential sprinkle of salt. Food means different things to different people and each person has their own 'rules' for making eating an enjoyable experience. It's not always enjoyable or pleasurable for those with autism. Food has the potential to create high levels of stress – and to be a significant worry for parents. Many parents basically want their child to eat *something*, to eat more food or eat different food, to eat with the family or to eat out. Simple wishes that can be difficult to achieve.

We have already seen how the sensory systems affect an individual's ability to tolerate social, physical and environmental demands, so we should foresee how any snack or meal is essentially an intricate recipe of tastes, textures, smells, temperatures and appearances, which may be hard to 'digest'. In some cases, children may avoid certain foods because they trigger an unpleasant memory from the past (and readers who have suffered with food poisoning must surely sympathise) but these memories may not be evident or meaningful to the parent, for example it was served on the wrong colour plate, a jarring noise was heard or a favourite toy was put away. In other cases, children may insist on particular colours of food like white or beige; they may avoid sauces and gravy, wet or mushy food; they may refuse to have more than one thing on their plate or to eat from the plate itself; they may insist on crunchy food or partitioning solid foods; they may not recognise when they are full and repeatedly ask for food, or they may only eat when their food comprises a specific number of elements – just like the child in the poem.

How we can help

1. If your child finds it hard to stay seated when she is eating, try to serve small portions of food each time so that it is easier for her to associate 'finishing' with an empty plate. Big platefuls can be off-putting and take longer to clear. If you want her to eat a specific amount of food, put smaller portions of this on a second plate and top this up once she has finished the previous one, and had a 'fidget' break. Over time, the portions on the second plate could be increased until the full amount is dished up in one go. While this may be onerous, it may make mealtimes more enjoyable – with less 'nagging' and fewer tantrums!

2. To encourage variety in her diet, think about the type of food she is currently eating and look for patterns, for example in the taste, colour or texture. Use these themes as a basis for extending the food palate, concentrating on the types of things she likes rather than those she doesn't. Some children will find it easier to accept a new food when it is repeatedly presented and when the goal of consuming it is broken down into achievable goals such as tolerating it nearby, touching it, putting it on a fork or spoon, smelling it, licking it, taking one bite and so on. Try to avoid giving her something different to try every mealtime so she has time to get used to a finite number of new foods before introducing others.

3. For children who self-impose strict routines around the food they eat, help them be more flexible by introducing visual aids. My suggestions include: a meal planner that you design together (the adult determines the options for the week ahead and the child decides when they are provided so she knows when to expect new foods or favourite foods), a calendar that schedules meals out, a self-serving bowl with a small serving spoon (showing how much food is available and giving the illusion of many helpings), or a Social Story™ that explains an important food rule (like eating from your own plate, using cutlery or putting leftovers in the bin).

Where we can go next

* James, L. (2016) *Autism: the restaurant steak that roared – video*. London: Guardian Online. Accessed on 03/08/17 at www.theguardian.com/society/video/2016/may/12/autism-the-restaurant-steak-that-roared-video

In this video, produced by *The Guardian*, Laura James (an adult mentioned in Part 1, Chapter 4) describes her experience of a meal out with her husband Tim.

* The National Autistic Society (2016) *Eating*. London: The National Autistic Society. Accessed on 24/01/18 at www. autism.org.uk/about/health/eating.aspx

This useful page includes reference to common problems, possible strategies and the services that can help.

69. It's Not the Same
(A poem about sameness of food)

Don't even think about it.
Don't you even dare.
Don't change my brand of yoghurt
As if I wouldn't care.

I'll tip it on this table.
I'll smear it in your hair.
Don't ever change my yoghurt
And make life more unfair.

What we can learn

I once did a training session for a group of staff wanting to learn about the sensory difficulties typically experienced by people with autism. I gave everybody a checklist relating to different types of food, materials, sounds and smells and asked each person to identify the things they liked and the things they hated. We fed back as a group and were amused by the intensity of our love or loathing of particular tastes or smells, often associated with particular situations. I made the point that we all have our own 'peculiarities' when it comes to food and drink, but that the way these are managed can be more extreme for an autistic person. So, if *your* favourite biscuits are out of stock on the supermarket shelf, you will probably settle for another brand or go somewhere else. If you run out of milk for your tea, you will probably make another drink or head out to buy a pint. In sum, you are more likely to cope with the alternative than to become distraught, you are able to see the 'bigger picture' and be flexible rather than rigid. This, of course, is not always easy for a person with autism.

In the poem above, we can imagine a parent who has been unable to buy the usual family yoghurts and opted for another brand instead, unaware of how this is about to be received by her child. In this case, the child tells us that she will become angry and upset – to her, the 'usual' yoghurt is the 'right' yoghurt, the 'only' yoghurt and the one that fulfils the routine she has come to expect, the routine that simply makes life predictable and the world right. To change the brand is to change the packaging, the texture, the smell, the taste, and even the very idea of what a yoghurt should be.

Those children who insist on a particular brand or type of food will be very sensitive to even the slightest of differences and won't be fooled! You could imagine that to offer Brand B rather than Brand A would be as distinct as someone serving you a beer when you'd asked for wine. Most unexpected, very confusing and potentially disorientating.

How we can help

1. For younger children, try introducing different yoghurts into messy play, so that they get used to the sight and smell of

them when they are feeling relaxed. Over time, you could encourage them to touch or lick the yoghurt on a spoon, gradually working up to a mouthful and then several spoons from the pot.

2. Try creating a reward chart that accrues points/puzzle pieces/blocks and so on each time a mouthful of new yoghurt or dessert is tried – potentially inviting the person to design the reward chart for herself. Start with small targets to begin with and work upwards so that she is expected to eat increasingly more of the food or to earn successively more tokens before the reward is given.

3. You could introduce a jar that contains tokens or coins representing the yoghurts or desserts available for the week ahead. Some, but not all of these will be her favourite. The desserts could be presented in a certain container so the child learns where they are from and can see them 'disappear' as they are chosen. The idea would be such that she pays for her choice each day using the tokens, choosing when she wants to have her favourite dessert but seeing that they are running out. The tokens could be transferred to a 'money bank', which can then be used to 'buy' next week's desserts.

Where we can go next

* Beckerleg, T. (2009) *Fun with Messy Play*. London and Philadelphia, PA: Jessica Kingsley Publishers

Tracey gives examples of how we can introduce wet or dry food in messy play – indirectly helping children get used to different types of food. You may want to use a special tray that indicates that the food you are using is for play (and is different to the food served at mealtimes).

* Koscinski, C. (2016) *The Parent's Guide to Occupational Therapy for Autism and Other Special Needs*. London and Philadelphia, PA: Jessica Kingsley Publishers. (Original work published in 2013.)

Chapter 3, here again, is helpful in explaining a variety of issues relating to feeding and eating, this time providing examples of activities that can be used to teach new behaviours.

Chapter 27

BEDTIME ROUTINES

70. Taking My Tablet
(A poem about going to sleep)

I like to have my tablet
As soon as I've been fed.
I like to have my tablet
Sitting in my bed.
The tablet makes me happy
And makes me feel alright.
The tablet makes me comfortable
And lasts all through the night.
But the thing about my tablet,
The thing that makes me frown,
Is when you take it off me
And when the battery's down.

What we can learn

Love them or hate them, touch-screen devices are part of modern day life and if you need proof of this, spend a few minutes 'people watching' the next time you find yourself waiting, queuing or travelling somewhere. It won't take you long to spot people using their smartphone or tablet and to appreciate why we have been tagged as the 'look down' generation. Simple to use, stylish, highly customisable, and operational in solo, they are naturally very appealing to people with autism. In Chapter 16: Fascinations and Special Interests, I provided some examples of how tablets can be problematic, and this poem supplies us with another example – this time in the context of sleep. It's a poem that could represent children young or old insisting on using their device for long periods before they go to bed (or in bed) and only stopping when the battery is flat or an adult intervenes. Teenagers, for example, may use their device late into the night or during the small hours when they can't sleep and may turn confrontational when challenged, not realising or denying its impact. Other children may make a particular game or film part of their night time routine and become incredibly distraught when this is interrupted, for example screaming, hurting themselves, biting, hitting out or throwing objects. In these instances, I can sympathise with parents who are sleep-deprived and/or stressed by their intervention efforts, but I still recommend that they continue: evidently children who sleep well, function well. My usual advice is to follow the conventional wisdom of avoiding electrical items in the lead-up to bedtime and to replace screen time with something more conducive to restful sleep in the long term. Many electrical devices are said to emit an invisible blue light that our brains associate with daylight hours (Alter 2017, p.69) and are, therefore, likely to affect a person's ability to fall asleep. A good time to change sleep routines is often in the school holidays when time is more plentiful and there isn't the pressure of the school or nursery run in the morning.

How we can help

1. If your child needs noise to settle at night, try playing music or audio stories softly in the background. These could be

matched to the cartoons, films or theme tunes that she has previously watched on her tablet.

2. Be a good role model. Try to establish a habit of using a tablet earlier in the day and in downstairs spaces, ensuring that there are at least one or two hours between putting it away and bedtime. Young children may be reassured by the tablet having its own bedtime routine, such as a special box or blanket that is used to indicate 'night night', and a consistent place from which to fetch it next time. The child won't then have to agonise about where it is and should be confident that she will get it back at the appropriate time.

3. Older children who find sleep elusive and are resistant to the idea of switching off their devices may need firm but fair boundaries and guidance; parents may have to steel themselves for some 'tough love' and explain why the instruction is necessary in terms that the person understands. If that sounds daunting, then you can perhaps enlist the help of your doctor – some children are more responsive to 'scientific' rationale and more willingly listen to medical professionals!

Where we can go next

* Alter, A. (2017) *Irresistible. Why You are Addicted to Technology and How to Set Yourself Free.* London: Vintage

An exploration of our fascination with technology in its many and modern forms. Chapter 10 is called 'Nipping Addictions at Birth' and discusses the negative impact of technology on children's interactions and communications.

✻ Walker, M. (2018) *Why We Sleep. The New Science of Sleep and Dreams*. London: Penguin Books

A brilliant book explaining different aspects of sleep and why sleep is important. Although it is not an autism-specific book, there are a number of references to autism and specific comments relating to teenagers that should be of interest. The author provides the reader with 12 top tips for sleeping, and many of these have relevance to children.

71. Dragons Under the Bed
(A poem about nightmares)

I have a special story
Which must be daily read.
It talks about me sleeping
Instead of jumping on the bed.

But…

At night my bed's a trampoline
Which gives me lots of bounce
THEY make me jump, so I will jump
Before they scare and pounce.

What we can learn

This is a poem about a child who can't sleep at night because she thinks there are monsters under her bed, although her parents assume it's because she wants to play. The first verse refers to the Social Story™ that they have written to discourage her from jumping on her bed. I usually have a great deal of success with Social Stories™, though they aren't a remedy for all children.

Certainly, they are less effective when their content does not address the real motivation for the behaviour exhibited. We can therefore surmise that the Social Story™ about bouncing on the bed is not really going to help this child in the short term; if she doesn't have help to manage her anxieties then she will always find it hard to go to sleep. Of course, this is not to say that bed bouncing is never about children misunderstanding what a bed is actually for; I have talked to parents of children who see the bedroom as an extended playroom rather than a place to sleep, or who use the space in a sensory way. Children in these categories may consequently 'resist' sleep by playing with the toys in their room, climbing on window ledges, clearing shelves, fiddling with light switches or stripping their bed of its covers.

How we can help

1. Sleep hygiene should not only concern night time routines, it should also be about the physical environment – changes here may help to relieve anxieties. If the room isn't comfortable relative to the child's needs, then routine alone won't be enough. Think about the number of toys in your child's bedroom and how accessible they are. Toys that are plentiful, scattered around the room and visible will only offer temptation or distraction. Think about the temperature of the room, the level of noise and the amount of light that your child would prefer. You may also want to consider the appropriateness of the furniture in the room – whether it is robust enough, whether it makes climbing more likely or whether there are too many pieces.

2. It may be useful to think about the bed itself. A child will find it difficult to relax if the bed isn't conducive to sleep. Consider, for instance, the pattern and weight of the bedding, as some children may prefer plain and/or heavy bedding. Some may

prefer to have their quilts tucked in tightly or reject them entirely. Some children may like to have a large bed or one that has raised edges, while others may prefer to use only the mattress and sleep on the floor. These things may challenge the conventional idea of what a bed should look like, but could improve your child's sleep (and be modified) over time.

3. Sleep interventions won't only involve thought about routines leading to bedtime or consideration of the environment, they will also include strategies for when your child can't settle. Persistence and consistency will be vital but stern friends. Repeatedly sending her back to her own bed (rather than giving in and moving over in your bed), consistently avoiding discussions (rather than indulging the problem with attention) and acting neutral (rather than seeming worried or cross) are all hard things to implement but will be more effective in the long term.

Where we can go next

* Jackson, L. (2004) *Freaks, Geeks and Asperger Syndrome*. London and Philadelphia, PA: Jessica Kingsley Publishers. (Original work published in 2002.)

In Chapter 4, Luke writes about the difficulties that many individuals have with sleep and suggests 20 ideas and solutions.

* Williams, D. (1999) *Nobody Nowhere*. London and Philadelphia, PA: Jessica Kingsley Publishers. (Original work published in 1992.)

In this autobiographical book, Donna intermittently makes references to her bed, sleep, night terrors and nightmares. On page 16, she talks of two imaginary friends known as the wisps (that hovered in front of her face) and Willie (the green eyes beneath her bed).

72. Tetractysaur

(A poem about routines and habits)

I
Just can't
Sleep until
The bedroom door
Is closed and I can have my dinosaur.
A routine bound by the three things we do,
Including when
My mum says
'I love
You.'

What we can learn

I wish I was better at taking my own advice sometimes, especially when it comes to sleep. Perhaps I should write a mantra for myself that begins, 'I will not sleep unless…' and make sure this does not include coffee late in the evening or checking my phone moments before I turn the light off. Time and again I convince myself that it's fine, that I am now immune to the effects of caffeine and blue light, and that I will not in consequence spend several hours lying awake in the dark wrestling with the 'I told you so' gremlin or turning about in vain attempts to get comfortable. As much as I think I need to indulge in these things (coffee and my mobile), I really don't – not at bedtime anyway.

Sleep routines are important for a good night's sleep but only if they are functional. Remember that routines often contain habits and not all habits are equal. So, while you may have established a routine where your 9-year-old son habitually sleeps in your bed (meaning that your partner has to sleep on the sofa), or a routine where your 5-year-old daughter has to have a dummy (that must be white), or one where your teenage child insists on surfing into the night, relatively few of us would agree that these are good habits or functional routines. Effective sleep routines should equate to routines that are straightforward and simple to carry out, which demonstrate self-reliance in the child, are not restricted by obsessions and which ultimately enable a child to sleep and rest well. Neat in theory but more difficult in practice. Imagine the child who has evaded sleep for several nights on the trot because you have decided to change an unhelpful habit (like removing the bulb so she can't switch the light on and off repeatedly). It would be easy to give in and revert to the same behaviour (allowing her to press the switch 30 times before finally climbing into bed), but this won't solve the problem and 'proves' that change is something to fear. Yes, changes can cause untold friction (arguments, tantrums, self-injury or destruction) but they needn't do so. Be brave, be mindful and be persistent. The pay-off might just be a good night's sleep for everyone.

How we can help

1. If your child's sleep routine is posing problems, think about the habits that she has developed and decide which of these are functional and promote independence (relative to her age and level of understanding), and which are unhelpful and breed dependence. If there are aspects that need changing, plan your approach and think about your timing – how and when you are going to tackle them.

2. Some children like to have a particular item in their bed and then suddenly decide that they have to have multiple and many versions of this item, to the point that there is almost no room for them! In this instance, give children a specific limit and show them where they can put the remaining items safely, for example in a 'special' box, lowering the numbers gradually where necessary. If your child is unable to count, you could define the number she is allowed by showing her the contents of a green box versus a red one (where the green box holds the ones that can be used and the red box the ones that cannot).

3. For children who insist that you repeat particular phrases for specific points in their routine, try using flash cards that show what you are saying and can be put away once said. In time, you could encourage flexibility by introducing choices of phrases, such as 'Shall we say "Pyjamas on" or "Time for PJs"?'

Where we can go next

* National Health Service (NHS) (2017) *How Much Sleep do Children Need?* London: NHS. Accessed on 25/09/17 at www.nhs.uk/Livewell/Childrenssleep/Pages/howmuchsleep.aspx

  Some guidance from the NHS website suggesting how much sleep children might need during the day and at night, according to their age from 1 week to 16 years.

* www.safespaces.co.uk

  Safespaces® provides special sleeping spaces or beds for individuals with special and complex needs, custom-made for purpose. While the specifications and specificity of the spaces mean that these are not inexpensive, I know parents who have accessed them, and the website includes information on how their purchase may be supported by funding. Other companies are easily identified through a search on the internet.

73. Toothbrush and Toothpaste
(A Poem about cleaning teeth)

Now the lid, next the paste
Squeeze it gently, do not waste.

Now the tap, next the brush
Make it wet, without the gush.

Now the brush, next the teeth
Clean the tops and underneath.

Now the paste, next you spit
In the sink, bit by bit.

Now the cup, next the gargle
Now your teeth can shine and sparkle!

What we can learn

This poem refers to the sequence of steps that a child is guided through each time she brushes her teeth – using a Now and Next board to highlight the most important points or to remind her of the appropriate behaviours. Many readers will already be familiar with a Now and Next board, but for those who aren't, essentially it is a visual aid consisting of two parts that name the first activity or task and then the second.[1] These parts are often

---

1   Some people prefer to call them 'First and Then' boards

represented (side by side) as simple photos, pictures or symbols and help to prepare the person for what is happening now and afterwards. Now and Next boards are a useful tool promoting a child's independence – teaching her to do something by herself, following steps much as we would follow a recipe.

Teeth brushing can be a challenge for many youngsters but poses particular challenges for those with avoidant or sensory-seeking behaviours. Some, for instance, can't abide the smell, taste or texture of regular toothpaste and refuse to have it anywhere near them, let alone in their mouth. Other children may struggle with the sensation of the brush or bristles against their teeth or on their tongue, and may not like the noise either. In other cases, children may like brushing their teeth but be more focused on details rather than processes. We can imagine that the girl in the poem, for instance, likes to squirt large amounts of toothpaste on the brush, that she likes to turn the tap on full and watch it running, that she may only brush some of her teeth or chew on the bristles, and that she may like to swallow the swill rather than spit it out.

How we can help

1. If you are using Now and Next boards to support daily routines, make sure you display them in a location that is accessible and relevant. You could have one for downstairs activities and one for upstairs activities (avoiding the confusion of going downstairs once ready for bed).

2. Some children may find it easier to use an electric (vibrating) toothbrush than a regular one; the vibrations could provide the sensory feedback that they require. From a (social) sensory perspective, children may tolerate your help more if you support from behind rather than face on.

3. Younger children who dislike brushing their teeth could learn to accept this in their play first, for example brushing teddy's teeth, and experimenting with different types of brushes and pastes. Older children could learn to tolerate it through graduated steps, for example starting with a mouthwash, accepting the smell or touching it to their tongue.

Where we can go next

* Autism Speaks (2010) *Dental Tool Kit*. New York, NY: Autism Speaks. Accessed on 02/02/18 at www.autismspeaks.org/family-services/tool-kits/dental-tool-kit

Autism Speaks is an American organisation founded in 2005. This source comprises its *Dental Guide,* a booklet containing information on how to help children clean their teeth and prepare for a visit to the dentist. The booklet also includes information for dentists treating children with autism and a pro forma that parents can use to tell the dentist what they need to know about the child.

* Multi-sensoryworld (2018) *Unflavoured Toothpaste*. Wirral, Merseyside: Multi-sensoryworld. Accessed on 02/02/18 at www.multi-sensoryworld.co.uk/collections/unflavoured-toothpaste

This weblink should lead you to a page which advertises a brand of unflavoured toothpaste called oraNurse® and gives a description of the product. I'm recommending it here because the lack of flavouring may make teeth brushing more acceptable to some children. I'll let you decide whether it is appropriate for your child!

Chapter 28

TOILETS AND HAND DRYERS

74. Toilet Training
(A poem about toilet training)

I cannot decide
Whether I like it or not
It's shiny and wide
I go there a lot.

Whether I like it or not
I have to sit there
I go there a lot
With my brown teddy bear.

I have to sit there
While my mum sings a song
With my brown teddy bear
I wonder for how long.

While my mum sings a song
My tummy gurgles inside
I wonder for how long
I cannot decide.

What we can learn

If you had one hope for your child, one skill or habit that you would like her to have mastered by this time next year, what would it be? To have a conversation with you or to sleep through the night? To eat a more varied diet or to spend less time on the tablet? Or would it be something to do with toileting? Toileting is one of those precious milestones that gives a child independence and makes one aspect of life a little simpler. Simpler is not always simple though; some children are only toilet trained after considerable patience, effort and ingenuity on the part of staff and parents. Incontinence doesn't factor as standard on the spectrum – some children master it quickly without any problem at all – but it can be part of more widespread issues that are physiological or sensory, social or psychological (e.g., anxiety driven). Commonly, issues may include pooing only in certain places (in a nappy, in the bath or in part of the house), constipation or holding for long periods (fearing the idea of letting go or the pain that may result). Where individuals are opening their bowels, they may not register this or, if they do, may try to hide the mess or try to smear it. Other children may become very distressed when they are changed, feel the need to strip completely before they use the toilet or have to strip when their clothes get wet. Some children may refuse to use public toilets or school toilets and only go at home with certain people around. Still other children (as we are about to see in the next poem) may treat the toilet as something it is not, as somewhere to play. I personally think that toilet training is more often successful with autistic children when their physical readiness is complemented by an appropriate level of social awareness. The toddler in the poem, for example, may be physically ready but does not distinguish the toilet from any other type of seat and lacks an understanding of the process she is being taught. For her, sitting on the 'white chair' is simply something she does at regular points of the day, holding her favourite teddy while her mum sings.

How we can help

1. Today's disposable pads and pull-ups are very absorbent and therefore worn with greater comfort for longer without the child feeling wet. Try dressing your child with her pants inside so that she grows used to wearing them against her skin and has the opportunity to feel wet in ways that might help trigger the toilet response (without causing mess).

2. For children who insist on wearing a nappy while sitting on the toilet or potty, you could cut a small hole in the pad so that their urine passes directly into the unit and so they can hear or feel what that is like.

3. Make sure your child can reach the floor with her feet (or a step if she likes to be off the ground) so that she is comfortable and her legs are not dangling in the air.

Where we can go next

* Devine, A. (2016) *Flying Starts for Unique Children*. London and Philadelphia, PA: Jessica Kingsley Publishers

   Chapter 9 focuses on toilet training in the context of school but the advice can be interpreted in more general terms for preventing problems and building independence.

* The National Autistic Society (2016) *Toilet Training*. London: The National Autistic Society. Accessed on 28/01/18 at www. autism.org.uk/about/health/toilet-training.aspx

This page, produced by The National Autistic Society, lists a number of topics relating to toilet training, which you can click on for further information.

75. The Magic Button
(A poem about using the toilet as a toy)

There's a magic thing in our bathroom
It's been standing there for years
If you press the silver button
A waterfall appears.

I love to press the button
To hear the water in my ears
And when I press it fourteen times
Amazingly, my mum appears.

What we can learn

Here is a child who uses the toilet for play, treating it like a cause-and-effect toy that totally absorbs her concentration and satisfies her interest in water. While the poem highlights the repetitive nature of her behaviour and her misunderstanding of the real purpose of a toilet, it also demonstrates the unique way in which people on the spectrum can view the world around them – and how this can lead to actions that are mistaken for bad behaviour. It would be very easy, in this instance, for the parent to think that the child should be told off before the toilet is broken and equally easy to see why this approach would not change the behaviour. It's another opportunity to emphasise the importance of reflecting on the motivation for the behaviour before acting. Our imaginary child, for instance, may need more structure in her daily routine so that there is less opportunity to engage in the behaviour, she may need to have appropriate water play built into her schedule, or she may simply need some specific toilet rules.

How we can help

1. Think about when and why the child is engaging in this behaviour. If she finds it hard to move from one step to another, use prompt cards and a timer. If you think the behaviour is sensory-seeking, create regular opportunities for alternative sensory activities: if she is fascinated by water, schedule times and places where she can play with it in a more functional way.

2. Use a toilet schedule that indicates each successive step of the process from entering the bathroom to leaving it, giving the child a focus that helps her use the toilet more appropriately and independently. The toilet schedule could be replicated on a portable strip that the child can refer to when she uses toilets in places beyond the house, for example with friends and family, at school or in public areas.

3. Try placing a card or tag near the toilet which reminds the child how many times she needs to flush the toilet (perhaps using a rhyme, code or list that additionally accounts for toilet mess that doesn't clear first time round).

Where we can go next

* Anderson, S.R., Jablonski, A.L., Thomeer, M.L. and Madaus Knapp, V. (2007) *Self-Help Skills for People with Autism.* Bethesda, MD: Woodbine House

Chapter 6 illustrates different ways of teaching a self-help skill and provides examples of how to shape appropriate behaviours, breaking the process down into small steps. The information could easily be applied to toileting.

* www.twinkl.co.uk

A good place to find printable toilet routines, available as posters, flash cards or mini timetables.

76. Dealing with Dryers
(A poem about hand dryers)

I don't mind using the toilet
I don't mind using the taps
But I do mind using the dryers
That blast like thunder claps.

The noise is loud and sudden
It frightens me deep within
What if my hands are underneath
And my arms get sucked right in?

So, after I've used the toilet
And once I've used the taps
I'll dry my hands on the back of your coat
And bolt with finger flaps.

What we can learn

Every now and then a story emerges in the media warning us about the volume of noise the average person is exposed to at work or about town, listing decibel counts and bemoaning the impact these have on our hearing and levels of stress. Imagine if those sorts of stories were shared on a daily basis. Would that make them more or less influential? Maybe it depends on who you ask. Certainly, for lots of people on the spectrum, noise is a very real problem – on a *daily basis*. Especially noise that is sudden, caused by someone else and has an unknown end point. Fire alarms and car alarms, thunder and fireworks, ringing bells and ringing phones, vacuum cleaners and hairdryers, barking dogs and crying babies – these are among the many that cause difficulty, but are they the worst? Not according to my conversations with parents regarding hand dryers and their capacity (whether in use or not) to prompt hands to ears, to invite screams and to send children running. The issues, of course, are not confined to children. Temple Grandin, for instance, is an adult with autism and, in her book *The Autistic Brain* (Grandin and Panek 2014), talks about the problem of noise created by someone putting their hands in the airstream. The sound of a hand dryer can genuinely cause pain to some; it is no wonder that they try to avoid them or feel unable to carry on with their activity once they are seen or heard. As a comparison, think about your automatic response to a balloon popping unexpectedly – how you startle and are briefly compelled to find the source of the sound. Now think about what it would be like the next time you were in that situation. The chances are that you would recall the moment, half expect it to happen again and then forget about it. You probably wouldn't continue to be affected by the memory, unless you were someone on the spectrum. The child in the poem is typical in her fear of hand dryers but here explains that it isn't just the sound that bothers her, it's also the worry that she will become trapped.

How we can help

1. Desensitisation can go a long way to helping but may take some time to achieve. Children cope better with noise if they can control it, so you could try recording the sound on an audio device and experimenting with its playback, for example playing it at low levels in the background while she is engaged in something enjoyable (changing the association she has with the sound). Try to raise the volume slowly over time. Alternatively, you could give your child warning that you are both going to listen to the noise but that she can choose the level at which it is played and when it is stopped.

2. You could teach your child to use a volume scale, which is a variation on the emotion thermometer mentioned in Chapter 7. Essentially, the two of you could design a scale from, say, 1 to 7 and label it with images, grading from sounds that are pleasant to those that are not, and add specific coping strategies. Once these levels are determined, you can use them to quantify the volume of public hand dryers (making the process more scientific than emotive). If your child finds 'level 4' sounds hard, you can reassure her by saying that the dryer is a level 3 sound and remind her of the level 3 strategy.

3. It may be helpful to practise using a particular hand dryer in a particular place, so that she is more able to predict the (specific) sound that may be heard and becomes more familiar with the physical environment. You could also practise using it at quieter periods.

Where we can go next

* Chalfant, A.M. (2011) *Managing Anxiety in People with Autism.* Bethesda, MD: Woodbine House

I have found this book useful when explaining the different aspects of anxiety and what Anne sees as the importance of 'encouraging bravery' (p.126).

* Grandin, T. and Panek, R. (2014) *The Autistic Brain*. London: Rider. (Original work published in 2013.)

Temple begins Chapter 4 with a description of her hatred for hand dryers and then goes on to discuss ways of categorising and managing sensory processing difficulties.

Chapter 29

TV SCREENS AND WASHING MACHINES

77. My-TV
(A poem about dominating the TV)

Quiz shows and soaps
Drama and news
Don't mind what we watch
As long as it's ME who can choose.

What we can learn

When I was in my thirties, I put most of my possessions into storage and spent a year volunteering overseas. I shared a flat with another volunteer and we made an unconscious decision not to have a television. It seemed unnecessary and we managed just fine without one. I held onto this habit long after I returned to England but was eventually drawn back in. I say this because watching television seems to be an inescapable part of everyday living – an activity as familiar and routine as having a wash or making tea – and one hard to resist once you see the contraption on. The television is often on in the background when I make my home visits, and while the children themselves may or may not be absorbed by it, they are usually very quick to notice when the parent changes the channel, adjusts the sound or switches it off. In these instances, the children tend to do at least one of the following: tug at the adult to correct the problem, throw a tantrum until order is restored, insist that the adult has the remote control, or attempt to fix it themselves.

Children who are fascinated by the television typically show their enjoyment in the way that they stand, the way that they move and in the sounds that they make. Children, for example, may stand very close to the screen (touching it with their hands, face or mouth) or yoyo back and forth according to the parts of the programme they like or don't like. Children may flap their hands excitedly or jump up and down on the spot. They may vocalise increasingly loudly or repeat exactly what they hear, including the accent, the intonation and the words. They may even like to watch the television upside down or perched up high. These behaviours might not only be triggered by an interest in the programme or a detail of it. They might also be due to the capacity of television to transport children away from social demands and to stream the sensory ones, collecting sounds and images together in one place. Plus, televisions have the added benefit of being controllable. If the child likes the pictures or sounds, then these can be quickly replayed, but if she doesn't like them, she can change them at the touch of a button.

How we can help

1. For younger children, show when the television is or is not available by using visual markers like a blanket or red and green cards rather than switching it on or off without warning. If your child fixates on the television, ensure that the first few switch offs are short in duration – so she learns that TV downtime is not eternal – and mark the time visually. Direct her to an alternative activity when the television is

switched off so that she can focus on or be distracted by something else.

2. Where viewing habits routinely cause conflict within the family, you may consider drawing up a planner that shows who can watch what and when. For early readers, this could be presented as a mini picture timetable, while for older children, this could be presented in words or in a personalised family TV guide.

3. If the television serves as a calming strategy for your child, consider ways of replacing this with a physical activity or a more portable resource. Physical activity will have a more functional and longer lasting impact, while portable resources make it easier for the person to self-regulate. You could try a space hopper, trampoline, a scooter, swing, bike or body board (i.e., a 'skateboard' you can lie on). Listening to music, drawing, reading or sitting in a tent-den may also be therapeutic.

Where we can go next

* Dyrbjerg, P. and Vedel, M. (2007) *Everyday Education*. London and Philadelphia, PA: Jessica Kingsley Publishers. (Original work published in 2002.)

Pernille and Maria here provide us with different ways of presenting a timetable to a child (with either objects, pictures or symbols) and show us how to create a cosy space in a small area, which may serve as a restorative retreat and an alternative to the stimulation provided by the television.

* Martin, N. (2009) *Art as an Early Intervention Tool for Children with Autism*. London and Philadelphia, PA: Jessica Kingsley Publishers

This book provides us with an alternative take on the term multimedia! It shows how art can stimulate creativity in young children and is included here as a replacement activity, or one additional to the television.

78. Remote Control
(A poem about viewing habits)

Hit fast forward and rewind
Repeatedly tap
Till the credits are primed.

Hit fast forward and rewind
Repeating movements
Are soothing I find.

Hit fast forward and rewind.
Your interruption
Is badly timed.

Hit fast forward and rewind.
When you take the remote
I pause the peace in my mind.

What we can learn

Take a moment to think about the best film you have ever watched and why you like it. Was the script brilliant or the scenery inspiring? Did it make you laugh or make you cry?

Were you taken with the soundtrack or a member of the cast? Have you seen it recently or watched it a dozen times already? Did you think the credits were amazing and feel compelled to study them over and over? I'm guessing that last answer will be a 'no'... While it's not unusual to watch things more than once, if you are a person with autism, your reason for doing so, the how and the why, will probably be different from someone without autism. Repetitive TV behaviours or a preoccupation with certain parts of the viewing are fairly common and children can become adept at finding the part they want, to the exact second. On a tablet, this may involve them homing in on specific YouTube videos and watching 'unboxing' clips. For some, it is about watching the movement of the credits (often shown on a plain background without 'social' clutter), while for others the joy stems from particular objects or particular phrases (including quiz show catchphrases). For still others, there may be relief found in knowing when the best bits will appear or when they should cover their ears. In some cases, children may *need* to watch a clip on repeat so that they can unpick it one layer at a time until the clip makes sense, for example studying objects in the scene on the first viewing, listening to the words on the second, then looking at facial expressions, then studying gestures and so on. This poem pays homage to children's viewing habits, reminding us of the importance of interpreting behaviours before we respond. It also alludes to the difficulty that children have in anticipating or understanding other people's intentions.

How we can help

1. Don't assume that you have to remove the behaviour altogether because you could in fact channel it and use it as an opportunity to develop communication and interaction, and join in with your child's sounds, words or commentary.

Do this gradually to invite interest not irritation. During your interaction, you can scaffold language by adding adjectives or verbs, by making your own observations or by asking specific questions. This type of support should develop her engagement with television and her response to you.

2. You could use the television as an incentive for a particular behaviour, for example introducing picture cards so that early communicators have to request the remote control or their favourite programme before they can watch it. Older children could be expected to do specific chores first, like clearing the dinner plates away or taking the laundry upstairs. (Ensure that children know what the chores are in advance and that TV time will follow.)

3. Establish realistic time limits for TV viewing – appreciating that the longer the interval, the harder it will be for the child to come away. Choose a suitable way of communicating these limits to help her understand and manage the time.

Where we can go next

* Kutscher, M.L. (2017) *Digital Kids*. London and Philadelphia, PA: Jessica Kingsley Publishers

   Chapter 3 looks at the impact of screen time and suggests why it is both appealing and problematic. The summary at the end of the book points out some of the advantages and risks associated with screen time, with reference to attention, play and violent behaviour.

* Normal, H. and Pell, A. (2018) *A Normal Family. Everyday Adventures with Our Autistic Son*. London: Two Rocks

Henry and Angela have a son who is 19 years old, and their book is a story about family life and Johnny's diagnosis. Honest and sometimes humorous, each chapter looks at different aspects of life on the spectrum and Chapter 19 is about routines, highlighting some of Johnny's viewing habits.

79. Washing Daze
(A poem about washing machines)

Round and round and round and stop.
Press the button at the top.
Round and round and round and stop.
See the bubbles fizz like pop.
Round and round and round and stop.
Moving like my spinning top.
Round and round and round and
STOP.

What we can learn

We can tell from the poem that this is a child who enjoys watching the washing machine and relates the rotation of the drum to other things that she likes or has seen in the environment. Though it is not the general rule, household appliances and objects that spin or rotate are often very interesting to people on the spectrum – perhaps from a scientific point of view (how objects and machines work) or from a sensory point of view (tuning into the noise, the colours or the vibrations). These objects can hold their attention for long periods of time and in ways that might be unexpected for their age or contrast with their usual span of attention. These interests, like others we have seen, may or may not be applied in a purposeful way. Children may not, for instance, fully appreciate what the object is designed to do and instead concentrate on one part (like a button, a hinge, the plug or a dial), using it as if it were a toy. So, if a child repeatedly pops the door open on the washing machine, she might be doing this because it reminds her of a pop-up toy. A child who switches the machine on and off might do this because it resembles her light and sound toy. Older children, however, may be more interested in the data behind the devices and become mini experts, acquiring innumerable facts, which they can relay at any point (whether the situation requires this or not).

How we can help

1. Show children how to use a washing machine properly and get them involved in the process where this is appropriate. Use a toy washing machine for younger children (shop-bought or cardboard inspired) and the real appliance for older children. It may be the case that they load the washing *and then* watch it spin.

2. Experiment with objects that spin or rotate to see which of these alternatives are of interest to your child. These may be items that spin under their own force (like a spinning top or a spinner) or can be spun by hand (like hoops, balls, ribbons). Items may also include those that roll (like soft play cylinders and marbles on runs), or those with wheels (like vehicles, toy trolleys, pushchairs, wheelbarrows and bikes). Children might also enjoy spinning themselves, say, in a soft play barrel, on a roundabout or on the spot.

3. Try to limit the amount of time that your child is allowed to watch the washing machine if this is one of her interests

– the longer the opportunity, the harder it will be for her to move on to something else.

Where we can go next

* Elder Robison, J. (2009) *Look Me in the Eye. My Life with Asperger's*. London: Ebury Press. (Original work published in 2007.)

John's accounts of growing up with Asperger syndrome demonstrate, among other things, his talent for taking things apart, fixing and improving them.

* Moor, J. (2008) *Playing, Laughing and Learning with Children on the Autism Spectrum*. London and Philadelphia, PA: Jessica Kingsley Publishers.

Take a look at the final chapter for ideas on how to challenge children's current play interests and manage their frustrations.

Chapter 30

FASCINATION WITH OR FEAR OF DOGS

80. Ralph
(A poem about dogs as toys)

Dog
Placid, playful
Running, panting, outpacing
How I love chasing
Ralph.

What we can learn

It is often said that a dog is man's best friend and we know that
our relationship with dogs has a long pedigree. We also know
that dogs or other animals can be hugely important to people
with autism[1] – providing therapy, creating an interest or forming
a career. Temple Grandin and Chris Packham are two great
examples from the spectrum. Temple is famous for her lifelong
work with cattle in America, while Chris is renowned as a
British broadcaster and naturalist working with animals. The

---

1   An interest in animals is not unusual in girls on the spectrum and notable because
    it can masquerade as a 'normal' interest

emotional importance of animals in Chris's life is evident in his fascinating documentary *Chris Packham: Asperger's and Me,*[2] – as we learn that he prefers the company of animals to people, that he contemplated suicide in his youth following the death of his falcon, and that his best friend today is a poodle called Scratchy.

Many of the children and young people I've worked with over the years have also displayed a great affinity with animals in real life or in their play. I have known people on the spectrum who love horse-riding, talking about fish or playing with dogs. I have known children become avid collectors of animal facts or plastic animals, plus many who insist on reading particular animal books at bedtime. I have seen toddlers lining up miniature animals or laughing with pleasure when hearing their sounds; watched children revel in the repetition of completing certain animal jigsaws and met others whose vocabulary regarding different species outstrips their day-to-day language. Though we shall see that children do not always regard animals in a positive way, animals do have the potential to reap enormous benefits – reducing anxieties, improving sleep, building interactions, encouraging communication and increasing wellbeing.

How we can help

1. A new pet is a new addition to the household and therefore brings new routines and expectations. Children may like the idea of having an animal but find it hard to comprehend the changes that come with it. Preparation for children is as important as preparation for the animal – explaining the care needed and how they can help (e.g., with food, bedding, exercise and play).

---

2   *Chris Packham: Asperger's and Me* (2017) [TV] UK: BBC1. You can also read about Chris's love of animals in his intriguing autobiography, *Fingers in the Sparkle Jar* (2016)

2. Involving the child in the care of her pet is also a good way of showing her that the dog, cat, rabbit or guinea pig is a living, breathing being and not a toy that can be mistreated or discarded. Establishing a routine that the child can feasibly be involved in should make something exciting and novel become a loved and respected creature.

3. Be aware of your child's ability to process and regulate sensory information to reduce the likelihood of overloading with excitement or frustration – for example, when the pet won't do what she wants – something that can happen if children are left to play with the animal for too long. Be mindful, too, of how the the child handles her pet as she may be heavy-handed or light-handed and not recognise the resulting signs of the animal being unhappy or agitated.

Where we can go next

* Carter-Johnson, A. (2016) *Iris Grace*. London: Penguin Books

  A true story highlighting the successes and challenges of a family raising a child on the spectrum. Iris's parents try a number of strategies and approaches to improve her engagement and these include contact with animals. The most rewarding relationship is the one that she develops with a cat called Thula.

* Isaacson, R. (2014) *The Long Ride Home*. London: Penguin Books

  An interesting account of a family's attempts to combat some of the more challenging aspects of their son's autism by taking him to healers around the world and educating him through nature. Rowan has a great affinity with horses and this is illustrated throughout the book.

81. Dogged Determination
(A poem about acting as a dog)

Once I've had my dinner
I like to wag and ruff
And jump across the furry squares
To dig out all the fluff.

What we can learn

If you were an animal, what would you be? A brave lion or a wise owl? A dark horse or a cunning fox? Presumably, most of us could imagine a creature with characteristics similar to our own if such a question came up in a conversation or quiz. I'm equally sure that many readers will relate to animals on an emotional level, cherishing pets as part of the family. Unsurprisingly, children with autism vary in their interest and attachment to animals and also in the way that they interact with them. Some may be wary or frightened, or conversely, be overly confident and unaware of the dangers. Others may view animals with ambivalence or follow them around. Some children will treat the family pet as a toy (trying to ride it or pull its tail), while others may copy its behaviour without realising how this is perceived. Dog play or acting like a dog is not unusual; I have certainly encountered children who like to crawl across the floor on all fours, bark or carry things in their mouth. It doesn't have to be regarded as a problem, though this might just depend on your perspective. What is cute for a toddler in the privacy of your own home is not necessarily so cute among public eyes or in older children, for example. Whether it is because children are fascinated by dogs, enjoy the attention or are trying to fulfil a sensory need, the reasons will of course be down to the individual. Strategies, however, will typically include focus on appropriate ways of interacting with pets (e.g., helping to feed, walk or groom), ways of structuring time and play (e.g., making toys available and planning games) and ways of managing the behaviour when it presents (deciding which phrases to use or avoid).

How we can help

1. Try making your child's interest functional by introducing animal- or canine-themed alternatives, such as reading stories in books, playing with toy replicas or watching programmes on screen. You could develop the interest further by teaching her about the wider range of animals and how to care for a pet (visiting pet stores, children's farms or zoos, for instance).

2. If the behaviour recurs but is fairly mild, try to reframe it as a sociable game, such as chasing or racing each other or completing obstacle courses in the garden. In this way, your child still reaps the physical movement benefits but is shown alternative and more varied ways of playing.

3. Where children appear to be fixated on dog or animal behaviours and you want to change these, think about the replacement behaviours that you will teach rather than simply saying 'no'. Decide on your approach and signal when the behaviour is or is not allowed, potentially complementing this with a reward system that trades stickers, tokens and points for a small prize.

Where we can go next

* Haddon, M. (2004) *The Curious Incident of the Dog in the Night-Time*. London: Vintage. (Original work published in 2003.)

Perhaps one of the most well-known autism books in recent years, this tells the story of a teenager with Asperger syndrome who develops a fascination with a neighbour's dog when it is mysteriously killed. The story reveals some of Christopher's strengths and difficulties as he tries to work out what happened – and inadvertently uncovers some family secrets.

* Kurtz, L.A. (2014) *Simple Low-Cost Games and Activities for Sensorimotor Learning*. London and Philadelphia, PA: Jessica Kingsley Publishers

This book has ideas for games you can use with young children who have autism (or another diagnosed condition). The sensory aspects of the games may be helpful for children who are interested in climbing, jumping or moving on all fours.

82. Pet Hates
(A poem about fear of dogs)

Racing through the park
Worried by dogs that may bark
Hate uncertainty
Sounds may cut me, sharp as teeth
Can't risk the growling beneath.

What we can learn

Misophonia is a word that Luke Jackson defines as a person's hatred of sounds; the word 'hatred' emphasising an intensity of feeling that goes far beyond mere dislike. Children, as we know already, are often pained by sounds in the environment, especially those that are unpredictable, variable in tone and outside their own control. It should come as no surprise then to learn that dogs are among the stressors that can impact on family life, whether that's seeing one on the television, encountering one in a park or the fear of meeting one not yet visible. Dogs can be a source of great interest to some children but cause significant stress in others. A large part of this anxiety may be due to the noise that a dog makes – that its suddenness is sharp and shocking and literally painful to the child's ears. It only takes one experience of this for the child to develop a thought habit, which then interferes with future meetings, with the child expecting all dogs to bark in this way and assuming that any dog must be avoided. Children may also be anxious around dogs because they don't like their smell, being jumped on or licked, because they have been hurt by one in the past or because dogs don't 'do' what they want them to do. Children, moreover, may not like the dog's tendency to walk all over their things or run off with one of their toys. They may also be upset by the dog's tendency to follow them around, not realising that this is a sign of interest and attachment rather than an intention to 'hound' them.

While these anxieties are not uncommon in the general population – a fear of dogs is known as cynophobia – in autism, they are compounded by those difficulties we know that children have in recognising and communicating problems and in thinking flexibly. Children with autism may take longer to overcome their fear than those without autism. The poem I have written portrays someone who hates the sound of barking, and concludes with an ambiguous line to make the reader wonder who it is that is on the verge of growling. Is it the dog or is it the child?

How we can help

1. Your child is going to encounter a dog at some point, no matter how carefully you plan your routes, so it makes sense to have at least one plan of action in mind – one that involves something you can say or do in a consistent way and, equally, something that helps your child communicate and know what to do. This may mean holding hands, taking deep breaths, or using particular phrases, songs and rhymes.

2. Some children may respond to a scientific approach to the problem, particularly if they like researching and sharing information. Learning facts about different dogs (e.g., about the range of breeds and roles they serve in people's lives) could help to change the way that they see dogs in the future – as an animal in nature rather than a creature to be scared of.

3. Consider present and historical reasons for why your child is anxious about dogs and use these as a baseline for addressing the problem. Then decide how the behaviour can be broken down into small steps and work towards each one in turn. If the reason is to do with noise, for instance, you might start by working on her tolerance of hearing a single bark in a sound book, in a video clip or on an audio tape (any of which she can control). You might then try to increase her tolerance to sudden barks in rough and tumble play or with toys, before moving on to real dogs (both familiar and unfamiliar).

Where we can go next

* Chalfant, A.M. (2011) *Managing Anxiety in People with Autism.* Bethesda, MD: Woodbine House

There are several pages in Chapter 5 that give specific examples of how to manage the fear of dogs in small steps.

* www.dogsforgood.org

   Dogs for Good is a charity that champions the relationship between dogs and people – using dogs in a variety of ways to educate children in schools, to assist disabled people at home or to help families of children with autism.

Chapter 31

SPECIAL TALENTS

83. Birthday Gift
(A poem about calendrical abilities)

Apparently, it's not good form
To ask the year a person's born.
'Happy Birthday' is hard to say
'Cos my brain thinks in other ways.
I know the days of dates I'm given
So, my gift to you is calendar driven.

What we can learn

I'd reckon that a quick search of the internet for information on autism would yield more results discussing the things that children need help with than the things that they can teach us. I'd also expect that information on the truly gifted in autism would be relatively scant. These gifted individuals are admittedly small in number but exist nonetheless. Referred to as savants, they are exceptional in their islets of talent. Their talents are almost indefinably remarkable, wholly uncommon and much much more than a special interest. Autistic savants will compare with others on the spectrum in terms of their fascination or preoccupation with the interest and the intensity of their concentration, but their level of expertise in relation to the interest will be far superior. So, while I have met a handful of toddlers who can sight-read, name geometric shapes and count to 100, I would say that these skills are remarkable (given their age) but not savant. Daniel Tammet, for instance, can learn a language in a week and recite the value of pi to many thousands of decimal places. He also demonstrates a calendrical ability, which means he can process the day of any date in history. If you gave him your date of birth, he could tell you in an instant what day you were born on. Knowing that such a skill exists helps us understand the poem in a slightly different way. Rather than seeing a child who doesn't say the 'right' thing, we can think about what she is saying, why she is saying it and what it means. Perhaps we have a child with a special talent that is hardwired to dates – that when she hears a date her first thought is about the day it relates to rather than the reason it was mentioned. It might also mean that the child is aware of her social difficulties but tries to mask this by talking about something she is more knowledgeable about, making her feel more at ease.

How we can help

1. There are many ways in which children can learn conversation skills and these can be scripted, to some extent, when based on common themes such as a birthday. One of the visual ways in which you can help your child with what to do or say is to use a set of picture cards or cartoons that show what the situation looks like to the people involved. The child could learn to read different types of body language and associate these with specific feelings.

2. If your child has a particular interest in or flair for something like maths, try to encourage it in ways that maximise its functionality. Children often have the ability to memorise information but not always the ability to apply it (such as

the children who can count in sequence but not relate the numbers to values). Make their interest part of an everyday range of practical activities so it isn't only demonstrated on the tablet, with the same blocks, the same book or the same person.

3. Try to strike a balance between nurturing an interest or talent, and over-indulging it. It's very easy to allow children to settle with something they like or do well and to encourage their talents with a sense of pride, knowing that it does wonders for their self-esteem and confidence. But it's also very easy for interests to become obsessions that make daily life tricky.

Where we can go next

* *Rain Man* (2004) [DVD] Directed by B. Levinson. Los Angeles, CA: United Artists. (Original film released in 1988.)

It's remarkable to think that this film is as old as it is, not least because it still remains in the public mind as a first base comparison whenever the word autism finds its introduction. It's an interesting film for many reasons, and especially because it provides us with an example of how autism and giftedness can influence perceptions and interactions – not only according to the person on the spectrum but also the individuals they are with.

* Tammet, D. (2007) *Born on a Blue Day*. London: Hodder and Stoughton. (Original work published in 2006.)

In this autobiographical account of Daniel's life from the early years onwards, he charts some of his challenges and achievements. You can read about his meeting with Kim Peek, a fellow savant, in Chapter 11. Kim Peek, incidentally, was the inspiration behind the character Raymond Babbitt in *Rain Man.*

Chapter 32

SOCIAL OCCASIONS

84. Party Popper
(A poem about parties)

Balloon
Filling with air
Soon to be deflated
If too much pressure's created
Beware...

What we can learn

I can't help but notice a subtle movement in the way that families are now describing their experiences of and attitudes towards social events. It seems that an increasing knowledge of autism is gradually changing parent expectations, with these focusing more and more on the needs of the individual than on convention, in that parents are less likely to feel the need to make their child conform just to 'keep up with the neighbours'. Birthday parties are a brilliant example. Parents who might previously have felt embarrassed by their child's behaviour at a party or upset by the lack of invitations – or even felt inclined to celebrate family birthdays in the traditional way – will now challenge people's judgements and reflect more on what is right for their child. Parents are not immune to silent stares and nudges but (I think) should be emboldened by the fact that their understanding of autism's challenges is deeper than that of the general public. So, in the context of parties, parents will be more sympathetic to the reasons why their child might refuse to dress up in special clothes and why she disagrees that it is a special day. Parents will know why crowds of unfamiliar people in an unfamiliar environment are difficult and realise that laughter and shouting may elevate anxiety. They will appreciate that the stop-start of music varying in volume and the presence of balloons popping without warning could cause distress. Parents will also be prepared for the outburst signalling that their child has lost in a group game or is trying to claim the presents that are not hers. Children shouldn't have to go to a party purely to fit in with their peers and please adults, but neither should they avoid them on the premise that something *might* go wrong. Instead, we should think about what children might enjoy and learn, and what might go *well*. Many children actually do like parties and look forward to them – typically when they are appropriately prepared and have previous experiences to go on. It also helps if their frustrations are managed and pressures remain low…

How we can help

1. Find out as much as you can about the party in advance so that you can make a plan. Choose the best time to visit (e.g., first thing before lots of children arrive or when children are eating) and decide how long you might stay. As ever, aim to leave on a good note so that your child is more likely to want to go to another one in the future.

2. Have realistic expectations about the child's engagement at the party and think about how you will help her with this, mindful of her age, interests, social skills and social understanding. Fidget toys, prompt cards, sensory aids,

timelines and sand timers may be part of your 'go to' resources for supporting turn-taking or sharing.

3. If your child is frightened of balloons then you can build her tolerance in small stages, showing her that balloons can be fun, for example looking at pictures of balloons in photos or stories, popping them on a touch-screen tablet, or inflating and deflating them in ready-steady-go games. Try experimenting with different sizes, shapes and colours to see if one is more appealing than another. If your child excessively likes to pop balloons, try redirecting her to alternatives such as water balloons, bubble wrap or balloon-themed computer games – or set a rule that says how many balloons she can burst and when.

Where we can go next

* The Guardian (2017) *The Party. A Virtual Experience of Autism – 360 Film.* London: Guardian Online. Accessed on 08/10/17 at https://youtu.be/OtwOz1GVkDg

   This link will take you to a short film produced by *The Guardian* newspaper which lasts a little over seven minutes. The party is experienced through the eyes of a teenage girl who becomes increasingly overwhelmed by social and sensory demands.

* Williams, J. (2016) *My Son's Not Rainman.* London: Michael O'Mara Books Limited

   John Williams is a stand-up comedian and a father of a child with autism. Chapter 19 is called 'Disco Fever' and – with humour and admiration – describes his experience of taking his son to a school disco.

85. Satdys
(A poem about weekend routines)

I love our Satdy mornings
When we go the shop
Me nan will buy a magazine
And I buy fizzy pop.

I love our Satdy din dins
Round at Macky Dees
Me nan will get a chicken wrap
And I get extra cheese.

I love our Satdy 'noons
With a movie from Netflix
Me nan will drink a cup of tea
And I drink pick 'n' mix.

I love our Satdy ev'nings
Reading with me lava light
Me nan will put her onesie on
And I say 'Love you nan. Ni'night'.

What we can learn

If you ask a group of parents what they love best about their child, you will – without exception – hear people talk about their child's sense of humour, her memory and how loving she can be. How soon those words drop into the conversation may depend on how much sleep was achieved last night... Autism doesn't stop children being affectionate or wanting to spend time with others, but it might mean that they show their affection or interact with others in different ways, possibly not in the way that we'd expect or in the instant that we want them to. This is why the familiarity of routines involving people and motivators is so important. It's obvious. As adults, surely none of us would choose to spend time with people who are unreliable – people who forever change their mind at the last minute when we make an arrangement and then let us down. We prefer to be with those who make us feel comfortable and share some of our interests, not with people who find our company irritating and with whom we have nothing in common. *Satdys* then, is a poem that embodies these very principles, helping us picture the relationship between a boy and his nan that has grown out of time spent together learning and accepting one another's habits. These habits are so familiar and so predictable that they are comforting and make life – for a precious moment at least – virtually effortless and very enjoyable. Yes, it's true that habits and routines don't come without a price and can cause problems (what if the shop is closed or there's a power cut? What if nan is unwell or the lamp is broken?) but those that work well make the child feel well. Children with autism who reach this state of harmony are more likely to show us exactly what they are capable of. Which is a lot.

How we can help

1. Routines are important to us all because they make life easier, more certain and more efficient in the process of 'doing'. However, routines don't have to be exactly the same all the time. It is ok to make changes here and there, now and then. Allow yourself this luxury of thought, particularly if you feel that the child has outgrown the routine or that it's no longer functional. I talked about this earlier in reference to sleep. While it can be daunting to change a habit, it may ultimately be kinder. Teaching children to accept changes in familiar

routines (that you have planned for) should help them be more tolerant of the surprises that crop up in everyday life (the things you have not planned for).

2. Some children need lots of guidance and preparation (e.g., plenty of warning, planners, Social Stories™, timers) in order to see a routine through, while others are satisfied by verbal explanation alone. Know your child and know the routine to decide how much support is necessary, when it will be provided and what it will look like. This may vary from one activity to another. Remember that the familiarity of a routine should give your child a sense of independence, so make time for her to follow through the steps and avoid the temptation of automatically doing things for her.

3. One way you can make subtle changes to a routine is by providing choices that help the child see that other options are available while still feeling in control. The choices can be given directly or indirectly, verbally or visually. For example, if your child likes watching *Toy Story 2* all the time, the choices could involve: watching *Toy Story 2* or *3* (rather than automatically fetching *Toy Story 2*), leaving *Toy Story* and *Toy Story 3* in sight (inviting curiosity), openly asking her to choose between two other Disney films (planting new possibilities), or choosing whether to watch the film before lunch or after lunch.

Where we can go next

*   Drew, G. (2017) *An Adult with an Autism Diagnosis*. London and Philadelphia, PA: Jessica Kingsley Publishers

    Gillan Drew is an adult on the spectrum. In Part II of his book, he writes about the ways in which autism shows itself in everyday life, and in Chapter 4, he provides advice on strategies that can help, such as drawing up lists and plans and setting goals.

* Jordan, R. (2001) *Autism with Severe Learning Difficulties*. London: Souvenir Press (Educational and Academic) Ltd

Chapter 10 addresses daily living skills and leisure at home. It reminds us how children on the spectrum can find it hard to occupy their free time and suggests how structure and routines help a child feel more at ease.

Chapter 33

GOING OUT

86. Houdini

(A poem about seatbelts)

My mum calls me Houdini
When we travel in the car.
I like to take my seatbelt off
Because we're going far.

I have a new one every drive
To me it's such good fun.
It only takes a milli-second
To make the thing undone.

The only bit I do not get
Is why she never claps.
Surely mum should be impressed
With my quick release of straps.

What we can learn

One of the traits associated with autism is the tendency for children to see the world from their own point of view and to act according to their own needs. This becomes a challenge when the behaviour is risky and the child does not realise or understand why. Refusing to wear a seat belt is a prime example.

In the *Houdini* poem, we have a child who likes to undo the belt and will try to do this regardless of the type that her mum installs. We can infer that she enjoys the challenge of undoing the fastenings but doesn't understand why her mum gets upset or cross. Children may feel the need to undo their seat belt because they don't like the idea of being contained in a small space or sitting with something across them. Remember that their sensations of touch can be far more sensitive than you'd expect. Other children may not want to leave the house, or become distressed by being in the car itself, trying to climb into the front seat or to open the doors while the car is moving. When I talk to families about car-related issues, I talk about good planning and helpful preparation. Since we can't be sure that when we tell a child where we are going this matches up to where *she* thinks we are going, it is sometimes necessary to explain this in a more concrete way, for example with objects, photos or symbols. Imagine the number of places you travel to in a car (or taxi). How will she know that this particular drive is to the supermarket, school, grandma's or the holiday caravan? Does she understand how long the drive will last and is she sure that there will be a return trip home? These questions and others may be unresolved or confused in her mind. Remember, too, that the purpose of many of your drives will not necessarily be for your child's benefit or be viewed as such by her. Helping her know where you are going and why could reduce anxieties and make the drive more enjoyable for everyone.

How we can help

1. It may help to desensitise your child to seat belts by practising with one in the house for short periods, using an actual seat belt, a weighted lap pad or a piece of material. You could encourage your child to sit with it for increasing amounts of

time while being entertained by something she likes, such as a favourite toy, book, twiddle or tablet. Later, you could trial the strategy while parked up in the car and then over very short journeys, helping her learn in less pressurised circumstances.

2. Think about the car environment and ways of making this the most comfortable for your child (e.g., music on or off, heater on or off, shoes on or off, people talking or being quiet). We all have our own driving preferences and know that these vary according to our mood; children are no exception.

3. Try giving your child something to do while you are driving. This could be an item that she can explore, a visual aid that she can read or a game that taps into one of her interests, for example counting the number of particular cars, playing 'I Spy' or journey lotto.

Where we can go next

* National Center for the Safe Transportation of Children with Special Healthcare Needs (2013) *Car Safety for Your Child with Autism*. Indianapolis, IN: National Center for the Safe Transportation of Children with Special Healthcare Needs. Accessed on 24/09/17 at www.preventinjury.org/getattachment/0a34fdf2-a75b-4dff-8629-adaf162dfbbb/Autism;.aspx

This is an American source that has practical and helpful information on travelling in a vehicle, and includes a resource called *Riding in the Car*.

* https://theplaydoctors.co.uk

You can use this site to search for visuals that may help your child when you are due to travel or when she is in the vehicle. As an example, I have seen a communication fan (suitable for young children) that has pictures illustrating key words for a car journey.

87. The Left is Right
(A poem about persistence in routes)

I like to walk along the wall
And touch the bricks so I don't fall.

Keeping left is such delight
'Cos then I know that I'm alright.

Must go straight and can't turn round
My reverse is an upset sound.

I like to walk along the wall
Without the crowds – that's best of all.

What we can learn

This is a poem about a child who has developed a particular way of travelling from one place to another – needing to keep to the left-hand side and to touch the adjacent walls as she moves. To turn around, walk on the right or use a different route is to cause significant confusion or upset. I frequently hear parents talking about children who behave in this manner – insisting on journeys that follow exactly the same pattern each time they go out, no matter what. It's as if children have an in-built satellite navigation system that only works in one way – that once a destination is identified and the route programmed, this must be followed without *any* deviation on *any* subsequent journeys, otherwise complaints will ensue. If, for instance, the road is closed, there's been an accident or you take a short cut, the child may panic, assuming that she is no longer going to the same place. She may start worrying about things she will have to deal with on the way and wonder whether she will ever get home again. She won't necessarily understand your explanation or want to accept it – as far as she is concerned, there is no other way and a change of plan is not an option.

A capacity to memorise routes, however, could be considered, alternatively, as a skill or strength. Children who learn routes in this manner tend to learn them very quickly, perhaps after only one journey. How many of you can do this, I wonder? If you can, are you also able to name all of the shops and buildings along the route, or state the number of animals in the field you pass? Can you list the sequence of signs or remember the date and weather on the first outing? If you are someone with autism (or just have a terrific memory), then you might be able to do just that and more.

How we can help

1. You could give your child a breakdown of a journey in pictures – pictures that embrace her particular interest (e.g., the speed limit signs, logos on buildings, animals she will see) and use them in a way that engages her interest. The pictures could be presented as separate images on a keyring, in a container or on a board. Practise using them on short and local journeys and add successively more, continuously encouraging her to find new things. Alternatively, you could reduce the number of predetermined pictures and use blank or surprise cards, which invite her to think about something

she might see and provide you with an opportunity to announce a 'surprise' (i.e., variation) along the route.

2. If your child insists on touching surfaces as she walks, consider whether this actually matters. She won't necessarily be putting herself at risk and if it allows her to feel calm, then perhaps this is a low to no priority behaviour. If it is problematic, you could give her a sensory object to hold or join in with her 'game', suggesting things to aim for, such as the fourth brick or the sixth post, turning the behaviour into something interactive as well as comforting.

3. Older children may respond well to Social Stories™ that explain why journeys sometimes have to change so that they are aware of what might happen and how they can cope.

Where we can go next

* Haddon, M. (2004) *The Curious Incident of the Dog in the Night-Time*. London: Vintage. (Original work published in 2003.)

   When Christopher goes to look for his mother in London, he finds the station he needs by walking in a spiral (which he describes on p.172) and later comments on the fact that while he can 'see everything' in a scene, most people only glance and 'never look at everything' (phrases used on p.174). It's a nice illustration of the capacity that children with autism have to memorise details.

* Lawson, W. (2006) *ASPoetry*. London and Philadelphia, PA: Jessica Kingsley Publishers

   In the chapter on childhood, Wendy includes two poems called *Change* and *Routine,* which have relevance if not equivalence in the context of routes.

Chapter 34

CROWDS

88. First in Line
(A poem about queuing)

I have learned a clever trick
Perfected over time
When I let out a mighty scream
My mum is moved to first in line.

It's useful at the dentist
And handy in the shop
It's useful at the doctors
And during toilet stops.

It's useful at the barbers
And at the NatWest Bank
It's useful at McDonald's
And at the taxi rank.

It's useful at the airport
And at the school front gate
Although it makes my mum act weird
The noise ensures we're never late.

What we can learn

Many, most or all of you probably have more sympathy and patience for (any) child having a tantrum in a public place than you used to, because I'm presuming that your knowledge and experience of autism to date renders you more likely to wonder why the child is upset than to wonder why she is being so 'difficult' *and* makes you less likely to scowl at the parent who looks embarrassed and under strain. You will especially have empathy for the stress associated with queuing. Queues, unfortunately, are an inevitable part of social life in all manner of domains, from the ordinary and mundane to the rare and unusual, and there will always be one that appears when you least desire it. We could avoid them but that wouldn't be helpful in the long term: queuing is something that children have to learn or learn to cope with. In simple terms, autism and queues are problematic because – notwithstanding the usual sensory challenges – there is no guarantee of being first (to be anything else but first is to 'fail') and because waiting times are variable (punctuality is often vital, and inconsistency is unsettling). Waiting time is often further compounded by the somewhat imprecise language that adults may use to reassure the child, such as 'in a minute', 'soon' or 'nearly there' – and we have already seen the difficulties that children have with time-related phrases. The child in this poem is someone who dislikes queues or waiting and will scream in protest.

How we can help

1. Use a Social Story™ to explain why people queue and how the order is determined. If your child insists on 'firsts', the story could introduce new ways of being first, such as standing in front of mum or dad, packing the first item in the shopping bag or sitting on the front row of chairs. It could

also state how she can cope if 'first' is not possible in the way she wants (deep breaths, counting, using a chewy chew etc.).

2. Devise a queuing routine for the places that you visit most often. This may involve using the same checkout, standing in a particular spot, holding a specific object, singing a certain song or saying a familiar phrase.

3. Your child might need an incentive to queue. Try rewarding positive queuing behaviour in a manner that complements her desire to be first, for example earning 'first prize' or a 'gold medal' for allowing others to be in front or ahead. These rewards could be verbal or real depending on the individual; some children will be content with praise while others will need a physical reward.

Where we can go next

* Gray, C. and Leigh White, A. (2002) *My Social Stories Book.* London and Philadelphia, PA: Jessica Kingsley Publishers

   Chapter 3 provides a range of Social Story™ addressing potential problems in the community and includes several related to queuing.

* Shaul, J. (2016) *Our Brains are Like Computers!* London and Philadelphia, PA: Jessica Kingsley Publishers

   Part 1 focuses on the importance of other people's thoughts and could frame discussions regarding appropriate queuing behaviours.

89. Bread and Milk
(A poem about supermarkets)

So now we're off to TESCO
I'll strip my clothes al fresco.
You can wander in the aisle
As I just panic for a while.

What we can learn

How many of us would honestly say that we enjoy or look forward to the humble food shop – squeezing it in around the school run, work, childcare or a spare hour in the week? It's certainly not one of my favourite things and it's probably not one of yours. Shopping is a demanding experience in lots of ways and some days it will be more tolerable than others. On the good days, you probably take everything in your stride and run on automatic pilot, but on the bad days, you will feel very quickly overwhelmed by those taken for granted hidden demands: do I need a trolley or a basket? Should I pick the branded item or take the special offer? Will I use the self-service area or checkouts? What bags do I use? And so on. If it's stressful for adults who expect, understand and tackle these demands, then we should expect it to be incredibly stressful for children with autism who don't – children who themselves are coping with hidden and obvious demands up against an environmental backdrop of sensory loaded information that comprises crowding, competing noises, visual distractions, temperature variations and different smells.

If children do cope with the physical environment, then they may have other problems when it comes to knowing socially appropriate behaviours. Typically, children may have fixed ideas about aisle routes (e.g., visiting specific ones in a specific order); they may expect and insist on certain treats; they may raid, clear or climb on shelves; they may not cope with waiting and queuing; and they may struggle with strangers (e.g., being over-familiar, or lashing out or screaming when someone looks at them). Shopping isn't a terrible experience for all children on the spectrum but it can be very difficult for many, especially when we lose sight of their stresses and our own. Stress is a hungry beast and is quick to feed on triggers. Preparation and explanation are evidently crucial and may even need to include store staff. If staff don't expect or understand what they see, it's harder for them to help or react in a useful way.

How we can help

1. Practise visiting a local shop during quieter periods and for short intervals, gradually increasing the time your child spends there. Successive intervals of time may involve: walking to the shop and looking through the window, entering the shop for a minute, walking around the shop and leaving, going inside to choose one item, carrying a basket and so on. This type of preparation should equip your child with greater resilience for trips in the future, when you tackle longer visits and bigger stores at busier times.

2. Try developing pre- and post-shopping trip routines so that she knows when shopping will occur, can predict when it will end, and knows what will happen next. The pre-shopping routine may include calming sensory activities to make her feel more at ease when leaving the house, as well as the usual visual preparation that helps her know where she is going and how she will get there. The post-shopping routine may also involve calming activities, or reward time – but

ensure that rewards and reward time are linked to the home environment rather than the shop itself.

3. Give your child a job to do when you are shopping instead of expecting her to trail around after you. Just because *you* know why you are going shopping doesn't automatically mean that she does. You could, for instance, give her a basket to carry or a trolley to push. She could search for items on a shopping list as part of a game, put the food into the trolley or load the conveyor belt. She could also carry some of the finished shopping in her own rucksack. Some of these activities will have sensory benefits but all of them will provide that much-needed structure.

Where we can go next

* Corporate ASDA (2017) *ASDA Rollout 'Happy Little Helpers' Initiative to Support Autistic Children During Their Shopping Trips*. UK: Corporate ASDA. Accessed on 24/09/17 at www.corporate.asda.com/newsroom/2017/09/12/asda-rollout-happy-little-helpers-initiative-to-support-autistic-children-during-their-shopping-trips

In the UK in 2017, the ASDA supermarket store started an initiative called Happy Little Helpers. It was inspired by a visual resource made by an ASDA employer (Jenny Barnett) who has a son with autism. You can read about the initiative and find out about her game by using the link.

* www.autism.org.uk

The National Autistic Society has produced a pocket-sized autism alert card with accompanying information that can be given to members of the public who misunderstand the behaviour they see. Some families don't like the idea of 'publicising' their child's difficulties so alert cards are very much a personal choice. However, they can be useful, not only in times of stress but also in situations to prevent stress. Alert cards are available from a range of sources, or can be home-made and personalised to the needs of your child.

Chapter 35

HOLIDAYS

90. Half Term
(A poem about schools holidays)

Half
Term is
Hard for me.
It's always been.
Weekends are strange with no lessons between.

What we can learn

I'd wager that there are numbers among us who feel a shade out of kilter when the school term ends and we are gifted a period of free time. Bodies and minds that have grown accustomed to the daily rise and fall of duties now have to be reprogrammed and settled into a new routine, one of our own choosing. I'd also imagine, however, that this transition is accomplished quickly and soon supplanted with leisure that is relaxing and restorative. Leisure is vital for all of us and people with autism are no exception. Many enjoy time away from classroom demands and return to school revitalised with systems reset. Others find time out of school immensely stressful because the pattern of days has changed (i.e., getting up at different times, travelling to different places, seeing different people or doing different things) and worries emerge about when the norm will resume.

Children will likely have more time to fill by themselves – in school, there is always something to do – but not know how to manage this unstructured time. This can manifest itself in higher displays of agitation or anxiety – and with behaviour that seems to sabotage the 'nice' things that families plan. While a trip to the beach or cinema may seem like a good idea, it is not usually where the child goes on a Monday, for example. Children with autism generally prefer routines and activities that are predictable and can latch onto certain aspects of these, which must be adhered to in order for the world to make sense. Half-term holidays do not necessarily fulfil these criteria – a sentiment implied in the poem above.

How we can help

1. Draw up a timetable that shows when school will break and begin again. Depending on the child's age and ability, this could be presented on a kitchen calendar or the calendar on a smartphone, in a personal diary or on a laminated sheet.

2. Try to develop a routine for holidays and weekends so that there is some element of repetition and structure. The detail will obviously vary according to the child, not just in content but also in form, as some children will need a high degree of structure whereas others will manage with less.

3. Some children may like to have a school project on the go, maintaining their connection to school in a more tangible way. This could involve 'homework' sheets or tasks based on lessons that they enjoy, or creating a photo album or video montage that summarises their holiday and can be shared with staff.

Where we can go next

* Cohen, M.J. and Sloan, D.L. (2007) *Visual Supports for People with Autism*. Bethesda, MD: Woodbine House

   Chapter 5 features ideas on how to help children understand the passing of time.

* Lawson, W. (2006) *ASPoetry*. London and Philadelphia, PA: Jessica Kingsley Publishers

   There are a number of interesting poems to read in Wendy's book that lend insight into her perceptions of time, change and routines.

91. Sky-High (With The Nephologist)
(A poem about going on holiday)

We're going on a holiday
To Euro Disneyland
I'm rocking with my headphones
And squeezing both my hands.

My brother says he's excited
To meet with Mickey Mouse
But what about our seven days
In a strange and foreign house?

I think I'll stay inside this plane
And in the second row
Looking through the window
Naming all the clouds below.

What we can learn

The family holiday. Surely a calendar highlight – that glorious free period of eating heartily and catching up on your sleep, of making new friends and trying new things, visiting new places and seeing new sights, doing what you want, when you want. In sum, a time when everyone is going to enjoy themselves and return home rested and recharged. Maybe. Maybe holidays are exactly like this for you and your family. But I doubt it. And I say that without even mentioning the word autism, for I've travelled often enough around the corner and across the globe to see that holidays with children and families are rarely perfect 100 per cent of the time. Children with or without autism are children first so the potential for sulks, tantrums, disagreements or arguments is high regardless of any condition! Autism just makes these more challenging when they happen – challenging in the sense of understanding the reasons, knowing how to solve issues and being proactive in reducing the chance of them happening again.

Lots of children with autism really do love holidays away from home, especially if these involve being outdoors and active. Some in fact thrive on the novelty and are happy because their interests are entirely complemented by the holiday. Imagine the child who loves playing in the sand or water having a holiday spent mainly on the beach and by the pool, for example. For other children, however, holidays are daunting and overwhelming, and the stress spots are obvious. The things that they are expected to enjoy are probably the things that worry them the most and worry them at home too. You only have to reread the first few sentences of the previous paragraph to remind yourself of what these are: new places, new people, different food, different routines, new rules and new demands. If your child has difficulty using public toilets at home, then this will probably be difficult on holiday. If your child is particular about the food she eats, then this is going to affect mealtimes while you are away. If your child finds it hard to interact with other children, then this trait will be evident in a new environment. A child's autism doesn't stop because you are on holiday, but nor does her capacity to cope. Her resilience, your approach and your preparation will be needed in equal measure. In the *Sky-High* poem, we are introduced to a child (with a special interest in clouds) whose behaviour suggests that 'high' can mean two things in this instance: referring to rising anxieties and increasing altitude.

How we can help

1. Think about how you are going to prepare your child for her holiday. Consider when you are going to tell her and how much information you will provide. Some children need to know far in advance, while others are best told close to the time of departure. Some children require lots of information but some only cope with a little. A visual countdown or calendar can help children track time (you determine the timeframe), while pictures, videos and leaflets help children appreciate more about what is going to happen when they are there. Be careful of the language you use when describing the holiday; be mindful of those literal interpreters, and make sure that you describe how and when the holiday will end, and what will follow after.

2. If you use communication or sensory resources at home, remember to take them with you. It's an easy trap to fall into, thinking that children won't need them on holiday because they will be too busy 'enjoying themselves'. If your child needs them at home in a familiar environment, they are *more* likely to need them when they are in a new and unfamiliar one. You should also remember to update any communication system so that she has access to images that relate to your holiday (think of it as her holiday phrasebook).

3. Make sure that you build quiet time into the holiday at regular intervals. Some children may need more quiet time than others but most will probably benefit from at least some down time. New foods, sounds, smells, people, places and experiences will not pass by her sensory system unnoticed. Know your child and be proactive in avoiding overloads – don't wait for her to feel overloaded before you act.

Where we can go next

* Disney (2018) *Services for Guests with Cognitive Disabilities*. USA: Disney. Accessed on 13/09/18 at https://disneyland. disney.go.com/guest-services/cognitive-disabilities

  The Disneyland website has a section that provides important information regarding accessibility for people with 'cognitive disabilities', and this includes practical advice about ticketing, queues and meeting points as well as links to videos, maps and timelines.

* Manchester Airport (2018) *Special Assistance at Manchester Airport*. Manchester: Manchester Airport. Accessed on 28/01/18 at www.manchester-airport-guide.co.uk/disabled-facilities.html

  A number of airports in the UK now have autism-friendly provisions, which may include dedicated quiet zones, fast track check-in procedures and special assistance. Manchester airport has produced information packs preparing individuals for a journey through any of their three terminals and these are available via this link.

Chapter 36

CHRISTMAS

92. A Christmas Wish
(A poem about Christmas routines)

I can't go in the living room
The green thing makes me heave
So, I'm sitting in the hallway
Hoping it will leave.

I can't go in the living room
It smells like rotten wood
So, I'm going to keep my coat on
And hide inside my hood.

I can't go in the living room
The lights make me all dizzy
So, I'm sitting in the darkness
Until my head's less busy.

I can't go in the living room
Shiny parcels make me scream
But I will ask Father Christmas
To bring my routine.

What we can learn

When Christmas is over and the decorations are packed away for another year, do you find yourself feeling (for a while at least) slightly disturbed by the way that the room now looks? That you've become so used to the tree being in its place, its sudden absence catches you by surprise for a few days, and the furniture – restored to its pre-Christmas position – now feels as if it's in the wrong place? Or even that the *whole* room simply feels wrong? If you don't, then maybe you just feel a sense of relief that life can resume without further worry over presents, cards, visitors or festive dinners, that everything looks tidy again and is in its rightful place. Either way, whether you are wistful or relieved, at least you know why and are not likely to erupt with frustration or bolt with anxiety. However, you might if you have autism.

For some children, the appearance of decorations and trees, cards and presents is as unsettling a feeling as that known to you once Christmas has been packed away. A room that was once familiar and predictable becomes a place that is unrecognisable and overwhelming. How can your child be certain that routines will carry on as before? How can she function properly when her sensory system is trying to process new smells, different food and unfamiliar objects? How can she predict that this is only a temporary arrangement and that things will eventually change back? Imagine what this does for her anxieties. Your post-Christmas relief will be nothing compared with hers. In my experience, parents discover that the happiest memories of Christmas are often related to moments of success rather than specific experiences (e.g., when their child tries the turkey dinner or opens a present for the first time). Christmas seems to be more satisfying when there is a focus on what makes the child happy and how this can be achieved, rather than on what convention dictates.

How we can help

1. If your child is the only member of the family who can't seem to cope with Christmas decorations, then you can compromise by providing her with at least one Christmas-free space – somewhere she can go to avoid the lights, sights and smells when it all becomes too much. This might be a pop-up tent, her bedroom, the playroom or an alcove under the stairs.

2. Try introducing the decorations over an extended period of time and encourage your child to help you where possible, rather than putting them up by yourself when she is out or in bed. If you allow her to join in and choose where new things are put, she should feel less of the shock and more in control of the environment. This advice can apply to school and nursery classrooms too.

3. You could create an alternative advent calendar in advance of Christmas, charting when certain things are going to happen, and make this motivating by including activities that you are confident she will like. This will help her know what to expect and when (e.g., buying a tree, putting up decorations, wrapping presents, seeing Father Christmas), and also show when these things will end. You could tag post-Christmas activities to the end of the calendar to reassure her that familiar routines will continue. The advent calendar could consist of numbered boxes with objects of reference or could be a grid with pictures drawn on. If she likes the idea, she may even want to design it herself.

Where we can go next

* Ambitious About Autism (2016) *Christmas Tips*. London: Ambitious About Autism. Accessed on 20/09/17 at www.

ambitiousaboutautism.org.uk/understanding-autism/christmas-tips

A short but useful insight into coping with Christmas as seen through the eyes of someone with autism (writing for the charity Ambitious About Autism).

* The National Autistic Society (2017) *Christmas*. London: The National Autistic Society. Accessed on 20/09/17 at www.autism.org.uk/Christmas

Some handy hints are summarised on this page.

93. The 'Santa' Clause
(A poem about talking to strangers)

So, I cannot give to strangers, but
can pay His £5 fee.
And I cannot talk to strangers, but
can chat while on His knee.
I cannot take a stranger's present, but
can bear His gift to me.
I cannot understand these rules, but
you don't seem to see.

What we can learn

If you have ever tried to write a Social Story™ about strangers or tried to explain the social rules around meeting and greeting, then you will know that these seemingly straightforward tasks soon tie you up in knots thinking about all manner of permutations, and unwittingly conclude with a vital piece of information forgotten or taken for granted. I like this poem because it shows how a child can learn a rule and get confused when the rule is 'bent'. In the world of logic and literalness, rules aren't meant to be broken or have shades of flexibility because that makes the world and its people unpredictable and even more puzzling than usual. The poem also provides us with yet another example of the children who are detail orientated, focusing on the thought that 'since I don't know this person, he is a stranger and I'm not allowed to talk to strangers or accept their gifts' rather than thought that 'this is Father Christmas and I can talk to him with my mum. Father Christmas gives gifts to children as part of his job'. Children with autism often have interesting views on Father Christmas or equally interesting reactions. Some children may insist on being the first in the queue and get upset when waiting is required. Some may find the enclosure overstimulating while others may feel claustrophobic and disturbed by the low lighting. The bolder and more socially uninhibited may think nothing of clambering all over the adult and pulling on him or his beard to see if he is 'real'. Other children may panic when they see him because they have a phobia about beards or glasses, or because they can't bear the colour red or velvet. Some may describe his appearance bluntly and announce him as a fake ('Santa didn't look like this last year') or demand rigorous and technical explanations of his worldwide deliveries. Various children may have concerns relating to the gifts themselves, producing lengthy lists of items that must be delivered, showing annoyance over something they've not asked for, or refusing the gift because they don't like surprises or the sound of paper being torn.

How we can help

1. Don't let your child be put off by bad experiences: you can both learn from them. So, if she was very upset last year

because the queue was huge, liaise with the organisers and find a time that is quieter, or a quieter place where she can wait. You may be also able to arrange a jump-the-queue slot, which would give your child the opportunity to enjoy the experience (and then work on queuing skills in the time ahead).

2. Christmas grottos are rarely going to be situated in quiet places but may be more tolerable with access to sensory supports such as ear defenders, music in headphones or a weighted rucksack.

3. Try wrapping children's presents in a personalised rucksack, sack, box or bag, helping those who don't mind surprises but hate wrapping paper.

Where we can go next

* Gray, C. (2010) *The New Social Story*™ *Book*. Arlington, TX: Future Horizons

  Chapter 5 is called 'Celebrations and Gifts' and provides a variety of stories that you may find useful, such as the giving and receiving of gifts, waiting to open gifts, coping with wrapped gifts and coping with disappointing gifts.

* The National Autistic Society (2016) *Too Much Information*. London: The National Autistic Society. Accessed on 14/07/18 at www.youtube.com/watch?v=Lr4_dOorquQ

  This is a short video clip demonstrating what information overload can look and feel like for a young boy walking through a shopping centre. Watch this and then imagine how much more intense this would be at Christmas.

SELECTED REFERENCES

American Psychiatric Association (2013) *Diagnostic and Statistical Manual of Mental Disorders: DSM-5*. Arlington: American Psychiatric Association. (Original work published 1952.)

Autism-Europe (2018) *World Health Organisation updates classification of autism in the ICD-11*. Belgium: Autism-Europe aisbl. Accessed on 20/10/18 at www.autismeurope.org/blog/2018/06/21/world-health-organisation-updates-classification-of-autism-in-the-icd-11/.

Batten, A., Corbett, C., Rosenblatt, M., Withers, L. and Yuille, R. (2006) *Make School Make Sense*. London: The National Autistic Society.

Donvan, J. and Zucker, C. (2016) *In a Different Key*. London: Allen Lane.

Fry, S. (2005) *The Ode Less Travelled*. London: Arrow Books.

Hewett, D. (2017) *About Intensive Interaction*. UK: Dave Hewett Courses and Consultation Services. Accessed on 17/12/2017 at www.davehewett.com/about-intensive-interaction.

Higashida, N. (2013) *The Reason I Jump*. New York, NY: Random House.

Hodkinson, A. (2016) *Key Issues in Special Educational Needs and Inclusion*. London: Sage Publications.

Jackson, J. (2004) *Multicoloured Mayhem*. London and Philadelphia, PA: Jessica Kingsley Publishers.

James, I. (2016) *Asperger's Syndrome and High Achievement*. London and Philadelphia, PA: Jessica Kingsley Publishers.

Klin, A., Jones, W., Schultz, R., Volkmar, F. and Cohen, D. (2002) 'Visual fixation patterns during viewing of naturalistic social situations as predictors of social competence in individuals with autism.' *Archive of General Psychiatry 59*, 9, 809–816.

The Lovaas Institute (n.d.) *Pioneers in Effective Intervention. Practitioners of Effective Intervention*. Cherry Hill, NJ: The Lovaas Institute. Accessed on 17/12/17 at www.lovaas.com/pdf/pioneers_practitioners.pdf.

The National Autistic Society (2016) *Too Much Information Campaign Report*. London: The National Autistic Society. Accessed on 02/02/18 at www.autism.org.uk/get-involved/tmi/about/report.aspx.

National Collaborating Centre for Mental Health (2013) *The NICE Guideline on the Management and Support of Children and Young People on the Autism Spectrum*. London: The British Psychological Society and The Royal College of Psychiatrists. Accessed on 21/03/18 at www.nice.org.uk/guidance/cg170/evidence/autism-management-of-autism-in-children-and-young-people-full-guideline-248641453.

National Geographic Kids (2017) *10 Top LEGO Facts!* UK, South Africa, Australia and New Zealand: Creature Media Ltd. Accessed on 30/09/17 at www.natgeokids.com/uk/kids-club/entertainment/general-entertainment/ten-top-lego-facts.

Norbury, C.F., Brock, J., Cragg, L., Einav, S., Griffiths, H. and Nation, K. (2009) 'Eye-movement patterns are associated with communicative competence in autistic spectrum disorders.' *Journal of Child Psychology and Psychiatry*, 50, 7, 834–842. doi: 10.1111/j.1469-7610.2009.02073.x.

Normal, H. and Pell, A. (2018) *A Normal Family. Everyday Adventures with our Autistic Son*. London: Two Rocks.

Packham, C. (2016) *Fingers in the Sparkle Jar*. London: Ebury Press.

Peters, S. (2012) *The Chimp Paradox. The Mind Management Programme for Confidence, Success and Happiness*. London: Vermilion.

Reynolds, K.E. (2014) *Things Ellie Likes*. London and Philadelphia, PA: Jessica Kingsley Publishers.

Silberman, S. (2015) *NeuroTribes*. London: Allen and Unwin.

Tammet, D. (2009) *Embracing the Wide Sky*. London: Hodder and Stoughton.

The Nation's Favourite Elvis Songs (2013) [CD] USA: Sony Music.

The World is Not Enough (2008) [DVD] Directed by M. Apted. United Kingdom: Eon Productions. (Original film released in 1999.)

Who's Afraid of Virginia Woolf? (1966) [Film]. Directed by M. Nichols. Burbank, CA: Warner Bros.

Wikipedia Contributors (2018) *Sticks and Stones*. Wikipedia, The Free Encyclopedia. Accessed on 02/02/18 at https://en.wikipedia.org/wiki/Sticks_and_Stones.

Williams, D (1998) *Somebody Somewhere*. London and Philadelphia, PA: Jessica Kingsley Publishers. (Original work published in 1995.)

ABOUT THE AUTHOR

Sarah Cobbe is an autism consultant and PhD student based in the northwest of England. She holds a master's degree in Education, awarded by the University of Birmingham, and has been working in the field of autism for more than twenty years. Sarah also has experience of working with lecturers and in-service teachers in Kenya and was recently diagnosed as an adult with autism. Sarah can be contacted directly at s.cobbe@icloud.com.